ELIZABETH HIGGINBOTHAM

VICTIMIZED DAUGHTERS

Gender & Society request
a review of 750 words
due by 15 July 1995

VICTIMIZED DAUGHTERS

Incest and the

Development of the

Female Self

Janet Liebman Jacobs

Routledge · New York and London

Published in 1994 by
Routledge
29 West 35 Street
New York, NY 10001

Published in Great Britain by
Routledge
11 New Fetter Lane
London EC4P 4EE

Library of Congress Cataloging-in-Publication Data

Jacobs, Janet Liebman.
    Victimized daughters : incest and the development of the female
self / Janet Liebman Jacobs.
        p.   cm.
    Includes bibliographical references and index.
    ISBN 0-415-90626-1.   ISBN 0-415-90922-8 (pbk.)
    1. Incest victims—United States—Psychology. 2. Personality
development—United States. 3. Fathers and daughters—United
States. 4. Gender identity—United States.   I. Title.
HV6570.7.J33   1994
362.7'64—dc20   93-39239
                                                        CIP

British Library Cataloguing-in-Publication Data also available.

To SBL, to my sisters, Beth and Ruth, and especially to my sister, Judith, and my daughter, Jamie, whose courage and integrity have been a source of inspiration and love.

And where the words of women are crying to be heard, we must each of us recognize our responsibility to seek those words out, to read them and share them and examine them in their pertinence to our lives. That we not hide behind the mockeries of separations that have been imposed upon us and which so often we accept as our own.

—Audre Lorde

Contents

Preface

When I first began the research for this book nearly a decade ago, public recognition of childhood sexual abuse was just beginning to emerge. In large part the current cultural awareness surrounding incest can be attributed to the work of feminist activists and scholars who sought to identify the nature of sexual trauma and to foster the creation of a society in which denial, ignorance, and secrecy would give way to a more conscious and honest appraisal of the prevalence of traumatic sexualization within the family. While these goals for change remain strong, I believe we are now entering a new era of public concern, one that is reminiscent of European culture at the turn of the century, a period of time in which the disclosure of the physical and sexual violation of children was met first with shock, then with horror, and finally with denial.

Faced with the devastating reality that families continue to be a place of danger and victimization in modern society, some have attempted to discredit those who speak out against incest and other forms of child abuse. Feminists, therapists, and victims themselves have all come under attack. The backlash to which I am referring comes at a time when victimization has become a media event, as newspapers, magazines, and television, in seeking to expose the awful truths of modern culture, search for victims whose stories can be told and whose painful life histories are thus forced into public consciousness. As a result, society seems to be suffering from what might be termed, "trauma overload," as revelations of sexual criminal behavior are met with doubt and disbelief, strong emotional reactions which are fueled by the sheer magnitude of the problem.

As a researcher working in this field, I am only too aware of the confusion and fear which accompanies the disclosure of childood victimization. None of us wishes that any of this were true, most of all the victims themselves. Research on incest is difficult to do precisely because of the horrific nature of the violation. As the concerns over credibility become the focus of the public discourse on sexual violence, we risk becoming a culture where denial obscures the need for protection and revictimizes those who have already suffered far too much. It is my hope that this book will help to further authenticate the reality of traumatic sexualization, thus contributing to a scholarly dialogue that seeks to reveal and understand the sources of abuse in contemporary society.

Acknowledgments

A project such as this could not have been completed without the intellectual and emotional support of colleagues, friends, and family. I would like to thank Michele Simpson for her help in locating survivors for this study and for her insightful suggestions throughout the duration of the project. I would also like to thank Gayle Quick Huffaker and Catherine Schieve, both of whom gave a great deal of their time and expertise in reading and commenting on the first draft of the book. Their respective suggestions resulted in significant improvements to the manuscript.

A number of individuals read and commented on portions of the book as the project evolved over time. Among these, I would especially like to thank Michele Barale, Valerie Broin, Cordelia Candelaria, Jan Lemmon, Louise Silvern, and Marcia Westkott for their advise and suggestions. In addition, I would like to express my gratitude to Donald Capps and Richard Fenn and the participants at the Center for Religion, Self and Society, Princeton Theological Seminary, who inspired me as the project was coming to completion.

A different form of inspiration was provided by the environs of the coast of northern California. In the summer of 1992, I spent four weeks at Sea Ranch where I shared my thoughts, my emotions, and my struggles with the Pacific Ocean, the rugged cliffs, and the sea lions and wildlife that lived outside my door. I am grateful for the advance from Routledge which made this creative space a possibility and for the continued support and encouragement from my editor, Maureen MacGrogan.

Closer to home, I would like to thank Joyce Arbib, Linda Ellis, and Robin Lopez who listened when I needed to be heard. In addition, I would like to thank Renee Kutash and Martha Leahy for their good humor and computer assistance as I struggled to learn WordPerfect. Their patience and help, along with the computer hotline, saved many a chapter that might otherwise have been lost forever in the unchartered territory of my computer software. Similarly, I am indebted to Amy Wagner and Diana Phillips who provided invaluable library help, and to Sheila Bolsover and Erica Bolsover for their assistance in typing and transcription. I would also like to thank Anna Vayr and Women's Studies at the University of Colorado for providing institutional support for my research.

I am especially grateful to my family, to Gary, my partner-in-life, and to my two children, Jamie and Michael. As the book progressed, my children went from childhood to adolescence and thus this work grew up alongside my daughter and son. Their wisdom and love, along with the support that Gary provided, sustained me throughout the research and writing of this book.

The lengthy list of acknowledgments would not be complete without recognizing the individuals who made the greatest contribution to this project. Foremost among those I would like to thank are the survivors who shared their lives with me, often confiding their deepest secrets, their strongest fears, and their hope for recovery and well-being. As a truly collaborative effort, I am deeply grateful to the respondents who gave so generously of themselves so that others might benefit from this research.

Permissions

"Reassessing Mother Blame in Incest," *Signs: A Journal of Women in Culture and Society* 15 (3): 500–514.

"Victimized Daughters: Sexual Violence and the Empathic Female Self," *Signs: A Journal of Women in Culture and Society* 19 (1): 126–145.

Excerpt from *The Dead and the Living* by Sharon Olds. Copyright © 1983 by Sharon Olds. Reprinted by permission of Alfred A. Knopf, Inc.

Excerpt from "Briar Rose," *Transformations* by Anne Sexton. Copyright © 1971 by Anne Sexton. Reprinted by permission of Houghton, Mifflin Company. All rights reserved.

Excerpts from Toni A.H. McNarron and Yarrow Morgan, eds. *Voices in the Night: Women Speaking About Incest.* Copyright Cleis Press, 1982. Reprinted by permission.

"Leda and the Swan" reprinted with permission of Macmillan Publishing Company from *The Poems of W.B. Yeats: A New Edition,* edited by Richard J. Finneran. Copyright © 1928 by Macmillan Publishing Company, renewed 1956 by Georgie Yeats.

Excerpt from *I Never Told Anyone: Writings By Women Survivors of Child Sexual Abuse,* by Ellen Bass and Louise Thornton. Copyright © 1983 by Ellen Bass, Louise Thornton, Jude Brister, Grace Hammond and Vicki Lamb. Reprinted by permission of HarperCollins Publishers, Inc.

Excerpt from "Daddy," from *Ariel,* by Sylvia Plath. Copyright © 1963 by Ted Hughes. Reprinted by permission of HarperCollins Publishers, Inc. and by permission of Faber and Faber, Ltd.

Louise M. Wisechild, *The Obsidian Mirror: An Adult Healing From Incest.* Copyright Seal Press, 1988. Reprinted by permission.

1

Introduction

All illicit unions with females have one thing in common: namely, that in the majority of cases these females are constantly in the company of the male in the house and that they are easy of access for him and can easily be controlled by him.

—Maimonides

Among the oldest known creation myths in the Western world is that of "The Creation of Vegetation by the Mother Goddess." Translated from an ancient Sumerian cuneiform, this myth tells the story of Ninhursag, the great Mother Goddess, and her consort, Enki, who challenges the power of maternal creation.[1] The myth begins in the land of Dilmun, an Eden-like paradise, where Ninhursag gives birth to a female child, Ninmu. At the sight of the young goddess, Enki becomes aroused by his daughter. He embraces her and they have sexual relations. A daughter is then born to Ninmu. Enki is again aroused by the new female deity. They too have sexual relations and she gives birth to another young goddess, Uttu. Once again Enki desires his daughter and offering her the gift of fruit, he demands entry into Uttu's "house." The myth records that once inside,

Enki took his joy of Uttu,
He embraced her, lay in her lap, . . .
With the young one he cohabited, he kissed her.
Enki poured the semen into the womb,
She took the semen into the womb, the semen of Enki.[2]

Out of this incestous union, plants and vegetables are created, but as they come to life, Enki seizes the young vegetation, devouring his own progeny.

Although this creation narrative dates back to 3000 B.C.E., the story of Uttu, her mother, and her grandmother is a myth that has meaning for a contemporary generation of girls and women. As the current research on sexual abuse suggests the extent to which father-daughter incest remains a significant form of family violence in modern society,[3] the myth of Enki and Uttu can be read as a timeless parable, revealing the enduring nature of the sexual exploitation of daughters in patriarchal culture.

The notion that not even goddesses are spared the trauma of sexualization has a contemporary parallel in the life of Marilyn Van Derbur Atler, a former beauty queen who received the title of Miss America in 1958. In a public talk given in Denver in 1991, she disclosed to the world that she too had been the victim of sexual violence, an incest survivor whose abusive father had been a great philanthropist throughout his life.[4] The image of Miss America as incest survivor has tragically become an apt metaphor that, like the Sumerian myth, speaks to the violation of female children irrespective of class background or cultural difference. It is an unfortunate truth that although women may be divided by wealth, by race, or by ethnicity, sexual violence and the trauma of incest are ties that bind women across generations.

With an increasing awareness of the extent to which incest impacts large numbers of female children, theories of development must now take into account the effects of traumatic sexualization on the personality formation of victimized daughters. The research that is reported here seeks to establish a framework for understanding the relationship between incest and the construction of the female self. Following the ground-breaking studies of Christine Courtois, Judith Herman, Wendy Maltz and Beverly Holman, Karin Meiselman, and Diana Russell,[5] among others, this study elucidates the developmental effects of sexual exploitation on the female child. In particular, the work of Courtois and Herman has provided a foundation for the analysis of sexual abuse that is presented here. Through in-depth interviews with fifty incest survivors from diverse backgrounds, a theory of personality formation is elaborated that examines the role that sexual violence plays in the development of the female self and gender identity. This work extends the prior research on incest by bringing together the disciplines of psychology and sociology, framing the study of sexual victimiza-tion within the context of male-dominated culture and patriarchal family relations.

Description of the Study and Sample Characteristics

The data for the study were collected over a period of six years beginning in 1985 and ending in 1991. The research began at a shelter for adolescent girls and was then expanded to involve survivors from a wide variety of settings in the Denver metropolitan area, including the University of Colorado, a women of color support group, and a high school for teen moth-ers; interviews were also arranged based on referrals from mental health professionals. The respondents were selected from varied settings so that survivors from diverse backgrounds would be included in the study. This approach is particularly important because as Carolyn Thornton and James Carter point out,[6] the professional research on incest tends to focus on white middle-class women while the more general information is derived from public agencies whose clients are disproportionately represented by disadvantaged groups. This study includes participants from both settings.

The sample population ranges in age from fifteen to forty-two; the average age is twenty-two. Sixty percent of the respondents are white, 25 percent are African American, 20 percent are Latina, and 5 percent are of mixed ethnicity or race. A little over half of the survivors across all ethnic and racial backgrounds were raised in middle- and upper-middle-class families, while about a third of the sample have working-class backgrounds. The remainder of the women grew up in families that live at the poverty level or below. With regard to sexual orientation, 84 percent of the sample identified themselves as heterosexual, 10 percent as lesbian, and 6 percent as bisexual. The extent and type of sexual abuse varied among the respondents and included fondling, oral penetration, and genital and anal rape. Forty of the survivors (80 percent) were abused before the age of twelve, thirty of these before the age of eight. In 90 percent of the cases the perpetrator was a father or stepfather, a finding consistent with other research.[7] Fifteen survivors reported multiple abusers, including brothers, uncles, and grandfathers. The majority of perpetrators were described as physically and psychologically abusive. In 20 percent of the cases, the survivor had witnessed a life-threatening attack on her mother by the perpetrator. These findings suggest that incest is often part of a culture of violence that pervades the family.[8]

The study was carried out in three stages, each of which was conducted by this researcher and involved voluntary participation on the part of the women. In the first stage of the project, potential respondents completed a written questionnaire designed to identify those survivors who would be willing to participate in an in-depth research project on sexual abuse and who had received counseling or therapeutic treatment for incest. The second stage of the research involved an initial interview with the survivor to explain the scope and goals of the project. During this interview, I explained to each survivor that involvement in the study might lead to a reexperiencing of the trauma she had suffered and asked each of the respondents to consult with her therapist to determine whether participation in the study would harm the recovery process. Further, for those who were no longer in treatment, I established that they had access to support services.

The third stage of the research involved in-depth interviews that lasted from two to four hours to gather each survivor's retrospective life history. The respondents were not required to answer any questions that made them uncomfortable and were told at the start of the project that they could terminate their involvement at any time. In gathering the retrospective life histories, a semistructured interview schedule was used. Each respondent was asked to describe her experience with the abusive family, including her relationship with the perpetrator and with other significant family members. Questions concerning childhood, puberty, adolescence, and intimacy were also included. In twelve cases, respondents sought additional follow-up interviews as their recovery process led to a greater awareness of their experience and the impact of incest on their lives. As these women, as well as other respondents, reported, their involvement in the project provided an opportunity to speak openly about sexual abuse and to begin to disengage from the shame and secrecy of victimization. Research on incest has emphasized that the secrecy surroundng sexual abuse contributes to the shame that the daughter experiences as a result of traumatic sexualization in the family.[9] To ensure anonymity in the reporting of data, names, places, and other identifying characteristics have been changed or deleted to protect the identity of the respondent.

Further, the sample population, while varied, is not representative of all abuse victims. Among those who are not included in this study are incest victims who have not received treatment or who suffer from chronic mental illness and therefore are prevented from leading functional lives. By contrast, the respondents for this research were drawn from a population of survivors who are aware of their victimization and who, for the most part, are engaged in a process of recovery that is geared toward integrating the trauma of abuse with their present lives.

The ethnic and racial diversity of the sample permits an analysis of difference as well as similarity among survivors. In general the findings of the research confirm prior studies on incest and race which conclude that it is primarily in the areas of disclosure and treatment where race and ethnicity are most significant.[10] Thus, Robert Pierce and Lois Pierce maintain that "although the act of sexually victimizing a child is no different from one group to the next, there may be variables associated with the intervention, treatment, or research process that will vary across groups."[11] In particular, their research suggests that racial stereotyping within the dominant culture frequently leads to minimizing the importance of victimization among women of color.

Further, Audrey Droisen's research on racism and anti-semitism points out that disclosure of incest is affected by the marginality of the victim's family and the family's relationship to an ethnic or racial community. In this regard she writes:

> Many children do not tell anyone about their abuse because they feel responsible for holding their families together. . . . So too children protect their communities. They don't want to add fuel to the fire or prejudice. They don't want to be disloyal. Children are taught not to tell family secrets in public. How much more do they feel this pressure when they know their communities are despised and they are telling someone who belongs to the group which is doing the despising. The doubled division of loyalties becomes too confusing; too traumatic for a child to bear.[12]

In keeping with Droisen's assessment, survivors from both African American and Jewish backgrounds spoke of their fears that disclosure would in fact reinforce racism and antisemitism. Further, the study indicates that religion, ethnicity, and race also inform the meaning that the victimized child attributes to the experience of traumatic sexualization. These differences will be explored more fully in the analysis of data.

Because sexual violence is found among diverse populations and groups, the perpetrators described in this study include professional men as well as laborers, unemployed workers as well as physicians, and ministers as well as college professors. In the majority of cases, the respondents had repressed all or part of the sexual violence of their fathers and thus the abuse tended to be recalled years after the original trauma had taken place. Many of the respondents therefore manifest post traumatic stress symptoms in which early childhood abuse is reexperienced through flashbacks to the original traumatic events. The prevalence of post traumatic stress disorder among abuse victims warrants further discussion in light of the historical controversy surrounding abuse-related trauma and the contemporary discourse on sexual victimization.

Post Traumatic Stress Disorder and the Effects of Repression

In the later part of the nineteenth century, Freud treated eighteen patients, six men and twelve women, suffering from what he termed hysteria, symptoms of personality dysfunction that he attributed to traumatic sexualization in childhood. Through psychoanalytic treatment, Freud became convinced that these patients had repressed painful memories of sexual trauma which, banished from consciousness, remained lodged in the unconscious of the victimized individual. In a lecture to the Society of

7

Psychiatry and Neurology in Vienna, Freud reported his "momentous revelation," acknowledging the earlier work of J. Breuer:

> If one tries in something the same way to let the symptoms of a case of hysteria tell the tale of the development of the disease, we must start from the momentous discovery of J. Breuer: that the symptoms of hysteria (apart from stigmata) are determined by certain experiences of the patient's which operate traumatically and are reproduced as memory-symbols of these experiences. We must adopt Breuer's method—or one of a similar kind—in order to lead the patient's attention from the symptoms back to the scene in and through which it originated; and having thus discovered it, we proceed when the traumatic scene is reproduced to correct the original physical reaction to it and thus to remove the symptom.[13]

Freud thus understood the process of psychoanalysis as a voyage of discovery in which the patient, working with the analyst, searches through memory associations to reconstruct the original trauma.

Even as Freud presented his findings to the Society of Psychiatry and Neurology, he anticipated the disbelief that would accompany his theory of hysteria. Along with the presentation of his findings, Freud sought to convince his colleagues that the experiences his patients had recovered from the unconscious were indeed real memories of actual traumatic events. In responding to the critics of nineteenth-century psychoanalysis, Freud stated:

> But someone else, less determined to reject psychological theories of hysteria, will when considering our analytical results, be tempted to ask what degree of certainty the application of psychoanalysis involves; whether it is not very possible either that the physician forces such scenes upon the docile patient, alleging them to be recollections, or that the patient tells him things which he [she] has purposely invented or spontaneous phantasies which the

physician accepts as genuine facts. . . . doubts about the genuine nature of the infantile sexual scenes, however, can be deprived of their force here and now by more than one argument. In the first place, the behavior of the patients who reproduce infantile experiences is in every respect incompatible with the assumption that the scenes are anything but a most distressing reality which is recalled with the utmost reluctance. . . . whilst calling these infantile experiences into consciousness they experience the most violent sensations, of which they are ashamed and which they endeavor to hide.[14]

Less than two years after the presentation of this important discovery, Freud reversed his position on the prevalence of traumatic sexualization. Maintaining that "such widespread perversions against children are not very probable,"[15] he further developed his theory of Oedipal conflict in which he now attributed the remembered scenes of violence and violation to infantile fantasies. This shift in interpretation, while embraced by many in the psychoanalytic community in the early 1900s, has in the latter part of this century become a source of renewed interest and controversy,[16] as current research on sexual abuse links Freud's original theory to the contemporary diagnosis of post traumatic stress syndrome among incest survivors.

One of the first studies of post traumatic stress disorder among victimized children was conducted by the psychiatrist Jean Goodwin, who framed her research findings within the theory of hysteria originally proposed by Freud.[17] Drawing a parallel between the incest victims she treated and combat veterans who had been diagnosed as suffering from post traumatic stress disorder, Goodwin found that survivors of sexual abuse, like survivors of war, suffer from anxiety, fear, flashback to trauma, and repetition of traumatic events.[18] In keeping with these findings, Herman, after extensive work in the area of victimization and trauma, has developed a diagnosis for "Complex Post-Traumatic Stress Disorder."[19] This diagnostic classification enumerates symptoms such as loss of memory of traumatic events, the reliving of the experience, and a preoccupation with the perpetrator, manifestations of traumatic sexualization originally identified by Freud. In elaborating the symptoms of post traumatic stress disorder, Herman distinguishes between states of reexperiencing the traumatic event and the numbing and dissociation which may also accompany prolonged and repeated abuse.[20]

Both the early research on hysteria and the more contemporary studies of post traumatic stress disorder suggest that repression is an adaptive response to the trauma of sexual abuse. In bringing to consciousness the memory of past events, the survivor copes with intrusive images, flashbacks to victimization, and the memory of violation that her body holds. As the protective shield of amnesia gives way to the reality of incest perpetration, the survivor longs for an explanation other than the terrifying knowedge of her father's betrayal and exploitation. Thus, as Freud so poignantly explained, she will agonize over and resist the truth, even as she can no longer deny the real source of her suffering.

Because the process of recovery lends itself to reconstruction, as fragments of traumatic events are recollected over time, the initial stages of memory recall are often characterized by a lack of clarity and specificity. For some survivors, fragmented images of abuse are the only memories brought to consciousness, while for others more complete traumatic events are relived, almost from start to finish, as if the intervening years had not taken place. The recovery of repressed material may take months or even years to complete, and generally the more violent the abuse, the greater the repression. Thus, among the twenty respondents in this study who reported having been raped before the age of eight, the tendency toward repression was especially strong.

In addition to the data provided by the women interviewed here, other material on trauma recovery and childhood victimization is derived from published reports of survivors who have written autobiographical accounts of the experience of traumatic sexualization. These published reports are an important source of information that contributes to an understanding of the effects of incest on the self concept and self perceptions of the survivor.

Applications of the Study for Feminist Analysis of Female Development

Over the last two decades, the development of feminist scholarship in the area of female personality formation has been extensive. Beginning with the work of Nancy Chodorow, Dorothy Dinnerstein, Jean Baker Miller, and Juliet Mitchell, the field of feminist psychology has grown and expanded to include a wide variety of perspectives on women's development.[21] A purview of the literature in this field suggests that feminist scholars are concerned primarily with two areas of study: the formulation of theories of the self in relation,[22] and feminist interpretations of Freudian psychology.[23] The work that is presented here takes an integrative approach, applying both the self in relation perspective and Freudian-based theory to the study of sexual violence and development. In particular, this research elaborates on the role that fathers assume in the formation of personality, an area of investigation that has received far less attention than the significance of mothers in the psychosocial development of the female child.

Because of the nature of attachment that develops between the incestuous father and the victimized daughter, this traumatizing relationship represents the most extreme form of the sexual objectification of the female child in patriarchal culture. Thus, some troubling aspects of the research findings are the similarities between this analysis and descriptions of female personality development among women who may not have experienced traumatic sexualization in childhood. In the characterization of the female self that is presented here, one may recognize aspects of a more universal gendered personality which emerges out of the cultural framework of male entitlement in the patriarchal family. As such, this study, while focused primarily on the effects of sexual violation, also contributes to a more general understanding of female psychology, as personality is shaped by the forces of male domination and the power relations of a gender-stratified society.

Beginning with the destruction of the mother-daughter bond in incest families, the analysis investigates the effects of idealization on the father-daughter relationship and the development of an empathic connection between victim and perpetrator. The identification with the incestuous father is then examined from the perspective of identity formation in childhood. A theory of divided consciousness is posited wherein the victimized daughter internalizes both the identity of the powerful father as well as a representation of self as powerless victim. The divided consciousness characteristic of the incest survivor is explored through the daughter's identification with the aggressor and the simultaneous tendency toward revictimization that underlies her idealization of the perpetrator. The analysis concludes with a discussion of the transformative aspects of healing through which the female self is reclaimed and reconstructed.

This perspective on male identification and father-daughter enmeshment will undoubtedly engender controversy, as the research on incest illustrates the extent to which victimized daughters are not only denied the right to bodily integrity, but to the very self that is at the core of individual and autonomous personhood. As a feminist researcher, I am aware that studies such as these emerge out of the subjective interpretation of data. While the ethnographic material reveals the reality of the respondents' lives, the theoretical content derives from the interpretive framework that is brought to bear on the life histories of the survivors. What is presented here, therefore, is one of many possible interpretations of the effects of incest, a form of violence that has many varied and traumatic consequences for the development of the victimized child.

2

⚮

Incest and the Destruction of the Mother-Daughter Bond

Few women growing up in patriarchal society can feel mothered enough; the power of our mothers, whatever their love for us and their struggles on our behalf, is too restricted. And it is the mother through whom patriarchy early teaches the small female her proper expectations.

—Adrienne Rich

One of the most tragic consequences of sexual abuse is the effect of incest on mother-daughter relationships, the primary parental attachment that underlies psychosocial development and the construction of the female self.[1] The most important studies of incest to date reveal that mothers most often become the focus for feelings of anger, hatred, and betrayal on the part of daughters who are abused by their fathers.[2] In this regard, Judith Herman reports:

> Whatever anger these women did feel was most commonly directed at women rather than at men. With the exception of those who had become conscious feminists, most of the incest victims seemed to regard all women, including themselves, with contempt.[3]

15

Similarly, Karin Meiselman found in her study of incest victims that 40 percent of the women expressed strong negative feelings toward their fathers while 60 percent were forgiving, with the reverse percentages being true for their attitudes toward their mothers. Thus, she concludes, as does Herman, that negative relationships with the mother prevail.[4] These findings are supported by the accounts of survivors in this study as well. The majority hold their mothers accountable for the sexual abuse. One white, working-class adolescent, sexually abused by her father since the age of ten, emphatically stated:

> I hate my mother. I have no use for her. The social worker wanted me to see her but I said, no way. . . . I never want to see her again for the rest of my life.

The turning away from the mother may in part be explained by the denial and lack of support that sometimes accompanies disclosure of incest. This explanation appears to apply to 16 percent of the cases reported here. Among the women in this study, eight respondents reported that their mothers had been directly confronted with the incest but took little or no action to protect them. One of the most painful of these cases is recounted by a seventeen-year-old African American respondent who became pregnant after continuous sexual assaults by her stepfather. Here she describes the lack of protection she experienced throughout her childhood:

> My mom, she believes me now to a certain point, so she's just waiting for the paternity test to be done. She says she'll prosecute but then she's kind of wishy washy. When I told her before when it happened, she said she would get a divorce, but she never did. It was when I was younger. My favorite teacher knew something was wrong. So he called my mom at her job and everything and then she got upset at me. She should have took care of it then. He denied it then and he's denying it now. He even stopped for awhile but then he just started again.

A second example of nonprotection was also reported by a teenage respondent who was physically and sexually abused by her stepfather:

> When he gets drunk, he's the kind to get too cozy. When I tell my mom—because I just told her about it a couple of months ago—she said it was because he was drunk. Everything that goes on is because he's drunk. I remember when I was a little kid, he always made me sit on his lap, while my brothers sat on the floor. Then he preached to us. I felt uncomfortable and I used to always scrinch up and my mom always got mad. She asked me, "Why you scrinching up all the time?" That's why I told her just recently.

One final illustration of nonprotection is provided by an adult survivor from a white, working-class background. While in recovery, this respondent discovered that her mother had ignored the warnings of an observant grandmother:

> When I figured out I was a survivor of sexual abuse, I told my mom I wasn't coming home for Christmas that year and I said it was because of the abuse. She said, "I'm not surprised." That's exactly what she said. And I asked her why and she said, "Your grandma thought she saw something once." I said, "What?" She told me that my grandma said that when my dad was changing my diaper he kept rubbing my butt or whatever. My mom had no emotion while she was telling me all of this. I said, "Why didn't you do anything?" She said, "I had so many things to deal with, I had your dad,"—my dad's a batterer—"I just had a new baby and I was trying to deal with my mom and you were just so young, I didn't think it would affect you."

The examples of maternal neglect and nonprotection which are elaborated here undoubtedly contribute to the mother blame expressed by victimized daughters. Yet, these cases represent only a small portion of the accounts of incest survivors, a finding corroborated by other research on disclosure and maternal

17

responses. Existing studies in this area indicate that daughters often do not disclose the abuse to anyone and that once incest has been reported, mothers frequently act to protect their children from further victimization.[5] Because violated daughters tend to hold the mother responsible, irrespective of her knowledge of the incest or her actual role in the perpetration of sexual violence, a more comprehensive explanation of mother blame in incest families is required. Such an explanation must take into account the structural relations of the patriarchal family that separate emotional and social power into feminine and masculine realms of control, a separation that contributes to the idealization of mothers and the rage that accompanies the discovery of her powerlessness in the face of the father's sexual violence.

Maternal Power and the Psychosocial Development of the Female Child

The nature and impact of maternal power in the family is a much-debated issue in the study of mothering in industrial societies. Theorists such as Diane Ehrensaft discuss female power in terms of the woman's domain:

> While men hold fast to the domination of the "public sphere," it has been the world of home and family that is woman's domain. Particularly in the rearing of children, it is often her primary (or only) sphere of power. For all the oppressive and debilitating effects of the institution of motherhood, a woman does get social credit for being a "good" mother. She also accrues for herself some sense of control and authority in the growth and development of her children. As a mother she is afforded the opportunity for genuine human interaction, in contrast to the alienation and depersonalization of the workplace.[6]

In contrast, theorists such as Juliet Mitchell reject the notion that women are powerful because of their central socializing role within the family, arguing that this approach mistakes isolation for freedom.[7] Despite their differences, however, these theorists share the common goal of establishing objective measures of power. As a consequence, they overlook the importance of subjective accounts of familial power relations. In order to understand the impact of incest on a child's relationship to her mother, the child's interpretation of her experience must be examined in relation to the dominant role of the mother in primary childcare. The concept of power within the family can thus be divided into the affective (emotional) domain of maternal control and the social (structural) domain of paternal control.

In this model, the prevalence of mother blame among victimized daughters can be explained through a feminist reinterpretation of the object relations approach to psychoanalytic development, which focuses on the significance of mothering in the formation of personality. Although object relations theory has tended to reinforce the sexism of traditional psychoanalytic thought, it is nonetheless useful to a discussion of mother blame in incest. The field of object relations, as it emerged through the work of Ronald Fairbairn, Michael Balint, and particularly Donald Winnicott, provided the basis upon which the phenomenon of mother blame came to be associated with explanations of family pathology that focused on the mother's personality dysfunction and poor emotional adjustment.[8]

In *An Object Relations Theory of the Personality*, Fairbairn maintains that the first social relationship experienced by an infant is that between the child and the mother and that "the nature of the relationship so established exercises a profound influence upon the subsequent relationships of the individual and upon his [or her] social attitude in general."[9] Having thus established the developmental primacy of the mother-child bond, he then elaborates on the stages of dependency through which the child passes as he or she experiences the mother as a source first of physical gratification (sucking and feeding) and then of emotional gratification (attention and affection).[10] Michael Balint argues that the social-relational needs of love and attention are as significant to the primary maternal relationship as are the more physical needs identified first by Freud[11] and later elaborated by Fairbairn.

These theorists maintain that the primary source of gratification, the mother, is perceived by the child as omnipotent, a powerful figure on whom the child is totally dependent from the first moments of life. The mother is both the object of love who offers total and immediate gratification and the object of frustration and anger when such gratification is not provided instantly or is withheld. The relationship that develops is therefore defined by dependency, helplessness, and ambivalence. Winnicott, like Fairbairn, focuses on the merging of infant with mother, explaining the relationship of connectedness not only in terms of the child but in terms of the mother as well. The adequate mother, according to Winnicott, fulfills and gratifies her child's needs through a process of "primary maternal occupation" in which she perceives herself to be merged physically with the child, a psychic state of relatedness that lays the foundation for the development of the child's ego.[12] Thus, Winnicott theorizes that splits in ego development, rather than an inevitable consequence of infantile frustration and anger, develop as a result of inadequate mothering. When the mother fails to merge with the child, fails to meet the infant's needs to the exclusion of all other concerns, the child is likely to develop a false self characterized by a splintering of the ego that interferes with emotional and interpersonal development.[13]

This analysis of infant-mother dependency, as Janet Sayers suggests, "hardly seems promising stuff out of which to forge a feminist perspective on psychology."[14] In this regard, Gayle Rubin has noted the danger inherent in borrowing from sexist ideologies in the construction of feminist theory.[15] Still, as Rubin points out in defending her own use of psychoanalysis, the work of the Freudians "enables us to isolate sex and gender from 'mode of production' and to counter a certain tendency to explain sex oppression as a reflex of economic forces."[16] In identifying the relationship of structural forces to family dynamics and psychological development, feminist analysis of object relations theory counters the tendency toward reflexivity without undervaluing the role economic forces play in forming and maintaining gender relations. In particular, the work of Nancy Chodorow has provided a basis for reframing an understanding of mothering and child development in patriarchy by linking the structural characteristics of child-rearing patterns to the role of the father in economic production.[17]

Chodorow, like Fairbairn and Winnicott, seeks to explain personality and ego development in relation to the primary bonding of mother and child. In her analysis, the father is a secondary figure in the emotional life of the child because his instrumental role within the family places him outside the sphere of emotional development and attachment. The patriarchal family, because it allocates sole responsibility for childcare and nurturing to mothers, contributes to the creation of a separate sphere of female responsibility on the basis of which mothers are judged to be either good or bad, successes or failures, both by society and by the child. In cases of incest, the child's identification and acknowledgment of the existence and importance of the affective maternal domain plays a crucial role in mother blame. That the child sees the mother as the most significant source of power within the family, irrespective of the social reality of the situation, is a result of the expressive role allocated to women as the providers of emotional needs and protection within the family.

Child development, as it is understood within a feminist framework of object relations theory, is not based on the adequacies or inadequacies of the mother, but on a structural arrangement of family relations that locates the mother in a central position with regard to the affective realm of personality formation. At issue, then, is not the quality of bonding *per se* but the structural conditions that define emotional development as exclusively the mother's province—conditions that legitimize mother blaming. The outcome of such structural arrangements, according to Chodorow and Susan Contratto, creates conditions through which

> blame and idealization of mothers have become our cultural ideology. This ideology, however, gains meaning from and is partially produced by infantile fantasies that are themselves the outcome of being mothered exclusively by one woman. If mothers have exclusive responsibility for infants who are totally dependent, then to the infant they are the source of all good and evil.[18]

Chodorow and Contratto are particularly critical of contemporary writers who confuse infantile fantasy with the reality of maternal actions and thereby contribute to the notion that mothers are in actuality all-powerful ominous caretakers whose control is real and absolute.[19] In the case of incest victims, however, what Chodorow and Contratto term infantile fantasy is in fact the subjective reality through which the child experiences her relationship to her mother. As a result, victimized daughters often confuse the true role their mothers play in the sexual abuse with their idealized expectations. The following interchange with a white teenager, which took place at a shelter for adolescent girls, is indicative of the child's subjective assessment of her mother's involvement:

Counselor: Why do you think your mother knew about the abuse?

Respondent: She just knew. I know she knew. How could she not know? We were doing it right outside the trailer and she was right inside.

Counselor: Did you ever try to talk to your mom about what
                was happening?

Respondent: No, I was afraid to tell her, I guess.

This young woman, like many others who participated in the study, was convinced that her mother was aware of the incest, although she never explicitly told her, nor had she witnessed her mother observing the abuse.

Similarly, a Latina adolescent, who also resided at the shelter, reported that she told her mother about her father's sexual advances but her mother had done nothing to prevent the abuse. When asked how she had explained the incest to her mother, the young girl said, "I asked her not to go to work at night. I said I didn't like being home alone with Daddy." When probed further, the teenager indicated that although her mother asked why she was uncomfortable with her father, she said she didn't know exactly but just liked it better when her mother was at home. The account of this young survivor is in keeping with the research findings of Grace Hubbard.[20] Her work with mothers of incest survivors reveals that, after disclosure, these mothers would recall that their daughters had often refused to stay alone with the incestuous father, a refusal that was later understood as an attempt to tell the mother about the abuse. Because attempts at disclosure are frequently misunderstood, the child may develop a deep and unrelenting conviction that her mother is aware of the incest and has therefore committed an unforgivable act of betrayal. Implicit in this notion of betrayal is the belief in the all-powerful and all-knowing mother who is capable of protecting the child from any and all harm.

Further, the psychotherapist Gayle Quick Huffaker points out that among African American women the sense of betrayal assumes a cultural dimension as well. Because of the historical roles of black women in the African American community, black mothers from diverse class backgrounds are often perceived, correctly or incorrectly, as the real source of power within the family, regardless of the roles that black men may actually assume. Thus, for the black incest survivor, feelings of maternal betrayal may emerge out of an idealization of mothers that is reinforced by the cultural realities of mothering in African American society. In addition, African American survivors also believe, and are frequently told by family members, that they should be able to cope with the abuse. As a result, black survivors who disclose their suffering often feel as if they too have betrayed the ideal of black womanhood, and thus they experience their pain as weakness.[21]

The issue of maternal protection among diverse groups of survivors is particularly germane in considering the part that fathers play vis-à-vis the sexualization of daughters in patriarchal culture. According to Miriam Johnson, the primacy of the mother in the child's emotional life is accompanied by the father's enforcement of sex roles:[22]

> Because of the initial identification of children of both sexes with the mother and because it is in connection with the mother that both sexes are inducted into "socialized" behavior, the maternal aspect of the feminine principle is seen as generic and symbolizing the common humanity of both sexes. The sex differentiating principle is introduced by the father. The woman's status as a sex object is related symbolically and ultimately to the father.[23]

The father accomplishes his socializing role by conditioning his daughter's sexuality, interacting with her as the prospective husband for whom she is ultimately preparing herself.

In Johnson's analysis of the father's sexualization of the daughter, she is describing normative family structures in which the sexual boundaries of the child are not violated. The incestuous family, however, places the father-daughter dynamic in an entirely different context. Where incest is present, the daughter's sexualization violates the boundaries of her physical safety and well-being. Issues of control and power in the family become more focused and intensified as the child's right to her own person is undermined by the father's sexual invasion. Such violations conflict with the child's assumptions about maternal protectiveness. The incest victim therefore experiences the powerlessness of women in the most personal and painful way, first through her own victimization and then through the knowledge of her mother's ineffectuality. The rage that comes to dominate her relationship with her mother is the anger of betrayal as well as the anger of deception, as the illusion of maternal omnipotence is destroyed in the face of the real power relations of paternal control and dominance.

Ann Ferguson thus characterizes incest as a form of male domination that destroys the mother-daughter bond by forcing the daughter's affective involvement away from the mother.[24] The effect on the mother-daughter relationship is twofold since the child turns against her mother even while her mother is powerless "to escape the oppressive economic, political, and psychological structures" of the patriarchal family.[25] Both Johnson and Ferguson conclude that any assessment of incest and the role of the mother must be considered in relation to the structural constraints of male dominance. Furthermore, Ferguson maintains that

> constraints such as economic dependence, legal restrictions on reproductive control, lack of strong female bonding networks that support sexual freedom for women or parental responsibilities for men, and physical violence by one's partner are all empirical factors that make women less free in parenting and sexuality than men.[26]

As Ferguson points out, domestic violence has a significant impact on mothering in incestuous families. Increasingly, researchers have become aware of the prevalence of wife battering among sexual abusers.[27] Among the respondents in this study, over half of the perpetrators were reported to be psychologically and physically abusive, creating an environment of fear and terror within the family. As one white, working-class survivor, twenty-eight years of age, described her father:

> The whole neighborhood was afraid of my father, that is no exaggeration, the whole neighborhood. He could be the nicest guy in the world but everybody was afraid of him. It was a horrible way to live. You never knew what he was going to do. Dinner wasn't ready, he would blow up; you didn't feed the dogs, he would blow up. You never knew. He has a lot of resentment and a lot of anger.

As this example indicates, incest is frequently part of a pattern of violence and aggression to which the child responds with anger at the helplessness that both she and her mother experience in the victimized household. Further, the child's anger at the mother is mirrored by the mother-blaming characteristic of male dominated society in general,[28] a cultural phenomenon that is especially evident in the prevailing theories of incest that attribute the sexual abuse of the father to the problems of a dysfuntional mother.[29] A brief review of the literature on mothering and family dysfunction therefore provides a sociocultural context in which to place the victimized daughter's rejection of her mother.

Incest and the Dysfunctional Mother

Social and psychological theories about the role of the mother in the incestuous family can be classified into the following categories: the mother as colluder; the mother as helpless dependent; and the mother as victim herself. As collusionary participant in the incest relationship, the mother either intentionally or inadvertently sacrifices her daughter in the service of her own needs. This interpretation informs two points of view about the mother's behavior.

The first view portrays the mother as "the family member who 'sets up' the father and daughter for the incest relationship, usually by withdrawing from her sexual role in the marriage and ignoring the special relationship that may then develop between husband and daughter.[30] The second view attributes a deeper and more selfish motive to the mother, maintaining that she actually derives unconscious pleasure from the sexual interaction through the voyeuristic role she assumes in the parent-child triangle;[31] or that the sexualization of the daughter helps her to achieve power in the family. The notion that the mother obtains power from the father's sexual abuse has most recently been put forward by Lydia Tinling who argues:

> The mother exhibits a dynamic process of her own in the way she interacts toward creating destructive elements within her environment, increasing the possibilities of incest. From an Adlerian position, one is convinced of the power she wields in creating her own fate and influencing the fate of others, particularly her children. . . . The mother who encourages incest, passively or actively, strives toward achieving her own personal and ultimate goal of superiority.[32]

Other analyses, some of which are more feminist in orientation, focus on the mother as a helpless dependent who is powerless to protect her child.[33] Her role in the incestuous family is thus understood and explained in terms of the power relations of patriarchal family arrangements. Aaron Hoorwitz describes the mother's ineffectuality in this way:

> In one variant of the classic [incest] situation, the father is a dominant powerful man, keeping his wife in a dependent helpless role. She may suffer from a disabling condition such as depression or physical infirmity. Although this may have been a reciprocal role relationship which satisfied both partners in the first years of marriage, the strain on the husband of his wife's dependency tends to anger the husband, who eventually distances his wife. He turns to a daughter, thereby obtaining emotional gratification.[34]

In this interpretation, it is the wife's dependency that leads the husband to engage in a sexual relationship with his daughter. A variation of this perspective is found in the personality disorder approach to family dysfunction. According to this view, women who are the subjects of oppression come to exhibit characteristics of passivity, dependency, and masochism. Meiselman describes the clinical data on this personality type as follows:

> In many incestuous families the husband is overcontrolling, emotionally cold, and even physically abusive in a manner that verges on overt sadism. We then assume that the woman must be extremely dependent on her husband and tend to attribute immaturity to her since her dependency needs exceed the adult norm, even for women. In extreme cases, especially when physical abuse is involved, the concept of masochism is invoked, evidently because it seems as if the woman must positively enjoy physical and emotional pain in order to remain in the marital situation. The term masochism is not generally used in its narrow meaning of deriving sexual pleasure from pain or humiliation; in this context, it denotes a kind of satisfaction gained from being a virtuous victim who suffers endlessly for her family and actively seeks to perpetuate her victim role in the face of well-meaning attempts by others to help her to escape from her miserable situation. . . . The three characteristics that we have been discussing—passivity, dependency, and masochism—appear repetitively in descriptions of the wives of incestuous fathers.[35]

Within the context of female personality disorders as described above, the mother contributes to incest through a role reversal wherein she becomes the dependent while the daughter assumes responsibilities in all areas of family life including the sexual realm.[36] This role reversal is reported by Herman who found that 45 percent of the sexually victimized daughters in her study had major responsibility for housework and childcare.[37]

Another variation on the theme of helplessness and dependency in the incest family describes the mother as the more independent parent on whom the father, in spite of his apparent dominance, is heavily dependent for emotional support. Mothers in this type of family are reported to be emotionally distant from both their daughters and their husbands, thus creating conditions under which the daughter becomes the surrogate wife and sexual partner.[38]

The third category of mother blame—mother as victim— takes a longitudinal view of incestuous families, maintaining that many mothers in incest families had themselves been abused as children. Their failure to intervene in the father-daughter relationship is, in part, a form of denial of their own childhood victimization. Margot Zuelzer and Richard Reposa maintain that for these women, "denial and repression of the realities of their family dysfunction and of their emotional pain is in the service of their own fragile self-esteem, and in the way they have typically learned to deal with unresolvable conflict in their early life."[39] Similarly, Hubbard maintains that denial is the most common defense found in mothers of victimized daughters:

> This seems to suggest that recognition of their daughters' sexual abuse would be to acknowledge their own abuse. This acknowledgment would arouse strong emotions that would be experienced as overwhelming and threatening. . . . To do so would force recognition of their own traumatic childhoods.[40]

Thus, the mother as victim of both a male-dominated family structure and her own abusive history offers a compelling explanation for the nonprotective parent; the mother who is prone to ignore or deny her daughter's victimization in order to maintain a thinly constructed sense of self-worth and the pretense of a tolerable reality. The identification of the mother's victimization also helps in understanding the frequency with which incest is repeated across generations,[41] as repression and denial prevents the mother from acknowledging the dangers to which both she and her daughter have been subjected.

In surveying these theories of mother blame, it is certainly possible to find the mothers described above in the reports of the survivors in this study: mothers who were abused and depressed; mothers who were withdrawn and emotionally unavailable; and mothers who lived in denial, unable to face the reality of their own lives or of those of their daughters. Although these maternal characteristics are not the source of the father's physical and sexual abuse, the victimized daughter, nonetheless, perceives these inadequacies as the violation and betrayal of the mother-daughter bond. Psychological survival thus becomes linked to separation from the perceived failures of maternal power. The result is hatred and denigration directed toward the mother. It is a painful consequence of mothering in patriarchal society that daughters in abusive families are forced to devalue their mothers, and women in general, in order to achieve a sense of self.

Indeed, some form of separation from the mother underlies the quest for autonomy for all children reared in a sociopolitical system wherein emotional bonding is the primary responsibility of mothers. The tension and ambivalence that characterize this separation are, however, magnified in the incestuous family, as disengagement from the mother is invested with issues of powerlessness and betrayal as well as the desire for autonomy and independence. The tension characteristic of mother-daughter relationships in general thus becomes manifested in its most extreme form under conditions of sexual abuse. In turning away from the mother, the child's attachment to the perpetrator grows in importance as the fantasy of the powerful and protective mother gives way to an increased idealization of the abusive father. In this regard, Herman writes:

> In her desperate attempts to preserve her faith in her parents, the child victim develops highly idealized images of at least one parent. Sometimes the child attempts to preserve a bond with the nonoffending parent. She excuses or rationalizes the failure of protection by attributing it to her own unworthiness. More commonly, the

child idealizes the abusive parent and displaces all her rage onto the nonoffending parent.[42]

Having suffered the loss of the idealized mother against whom she has directed her anger and rage, the daughter must now preserve the idealized image of the incestuous father. The idealization of the perpetrator thus becomes crucial for the psychological survival of the daughter who turns toward the abuser in her struggle to define the female self.

3

~

Idealization of the Perpetrator

I have always been scared of *you*
With your Luftwaffe, your gobbledygoo
And your neat mustache
And your Aryan eye, bright blue.
Panzer-man, panzer-man, O You

—Sylvia Plath, "Daddy"

The idealization of the perpetrator by the daughter in incest families is informed in part by the idealization of fathers in patriarchal culture. Theorists such as Juliet Mitchell suggest that the power which men possess in the public realms of law and religion is manifested in the internalization of the ideal patriarch in the unconscious of individuals. Writing in *Psychoanalysis and Feminism*, Mitchell maintains that:

> The father, in the context of the Oedipus complex, is not a part of a dyadic relationship of mother and child, but a third term. The self and the other of the mother-and-child has its duality broken by the intervention of this third term, one who here represents all that is essential to society—its laws.[1]

According to this view, the idealization of the father results from the merging of the symbolic patriarch of the unconscious with the real father who maintains control over the family.

For children this idealization is both social and psychological in origin as the social roles of men support their image of strength, competency, and value in the world, while the psychological needs of childhood dependency attribute kindness, love, and protection to the idealized father. This form of patriarchal idealization is demonstrated in perceptions of the father as capable, caretaking, and effectual in the world. As one respondent, twenty-nine years of age, explained:

> He always seemed to be assertive. He carries himself like he is powerful, as though he could get things done. And he does. He's always been, "Let me take care of everything. . . ." When I was younger I think I looked up to him in a way, kind of this distant powerful person who's always smartly dressed, and always impressive sounding. He's very articulate and sounds like he knows what he is talking about.

Contemporary feminist theory has stressed that the idealization of the father is enhanced by his absence from the emotional and social life of the daughter.[2] With the incestuous father, however, it is the dangerous presence of the perpetrator that intensifies the need for idealization. For abused daughters in particular the need to believe in the ideal father is especially strong as the extent of his control and the threat of his abuse violate the basic needs of trust and security upon which healthy psychological development relies. Thus, as Robert Summit concludes, the abused child is faced with the challenge of accommodation as she seeks to reconcile dependency needs with the reality of the dangerous father:

> The healthy, normal, emotionally resilient child will learn to accommodate to the reality of continuing sexual abuse. There is the challenge of accommodating not only to escalating demands but to an increasing consciousness of betrayal and objectification

by someone who is ordinarily idealized as a protective, altruistic, loving, parental figure.[3]

To sustain the ideal of the abusive parent the victimized child will often develop a range of psychological responses that help to preserve her sense of security and well-being in the face of an untenable reality. Among these responses, repression and self-blame are two adaptations through which the child reconstructs the abuse, thereby preserving the image of the idealized parent. Each of these accommodations to incest perpetration will be discussed as they inform the development of the female self and the child's attachment to the perpetrator.

Repression and Distortion as a Response to Victimization

Research on childhood sexual abuse over the last decade has documented the prevalence of repressed memory in incest survivors who suffer from a form of post traumatic stress disorder (PTSD) similar to that found in combat veterans and rape victims.[4] Among the symptoms of this disorder are fear, flashback to the trauma, and sleep disorders. These psychological manifestations of sexual abuse may be present in the child as well as in adult survivors, even when the actual experience of violation has been repressed, that is, withheld or expelled from conscious memory.[5] Thus, the victim may have an extreme fear of the dark or of intrusion without knowing who or what is the object of her terror.

One result of repression is that the identity of the perpetrator may be buried deep in the unconscious, while the trauma of victimization is manifested in psychological distortions which act as screen memories that are symptoms of an abusive history. These distortions can therefore be understood as a form of projection wherein the violence and aggression of the perpetrator are at once banished from consciousness and projected onto the outside world.[6] Thus, in the terror-filled reality of the abused child, the father may be reconstructed as a shadow figure or a faceless intruder, a malevolent presence that the child fears but cannot name.

Because sexual abuse often takes place at night when the child is between sleep and waking consciousness, the masking of the perpetrator's true identity is facilitated by the darkness as she becomes most vulnerable in her bed amidst the shapes and shadows which signal danger and intrusion. With the masking of the perpetrator's identity, a distorted reality emerges out of the trauma of victimization, a distortion which, according to Karin Meiselman, contains "glimmerings of repressed material."[7] The form and imagery that these distortions take vary across survivors and are influenced by the sociocultural environment of the incestuous family. For some children the evil which lurks in the shadow of their lives may be a faceless stranger who hovers over their bed at night. For others, raised in religious households where rigid definitions of sin and godliness prevail, it might be the devil who enters the child's bedroom and from whom she is not safe; and still for other daughters, the feared intruder may be an alien being or a Nazi soldier. These imaginery perpetrators emerge in response to the overwhelming reality of the father's violence and his sexual assault. A white, middle-class survivor, thirty-five years of age, offered this recovered memory of the menacing "ouch ouch body man" who tormented both her and her sister:

> When I was very young, and I shared a room with my sister, I must have been 3, 4, or 5. . . . I remember having these sort of erotic fantasies. They happened every night before I went to bed, and my sister had the same thing, and we were being sort of sexually abused, and we called the man, the figure that did it, the ouch ouch body man. . . . I remember being in bed and having this man kind of come up and do explorations on my body and sometimes put substances on my vagina that sort of tingled or burned or

something, like Ben Gay, different things. My image of it was like a dream that would happen. And maybe it was my father, because it was a man in uniform. . . . And my sister would have the same sort of dreams, or memories, or images, and we would talk the next morning, "what happened to you with the ouch ouch body man?" . . . Now I'm seeing and I have made the link that it could have been my father, it could have very likely been my father.

The uniform that figures prominently in these memories is significant for this respondent whose father was in the military throughout her childhood. When this respondent entered young adulthood, the screen memory was transformed by her belief that she had been a Holocaust victim in a past life, once again envisioning her tormenters as men in uniform:

I also link it [the abuse] to many of the memories I have from living in Germany, . . . all the memories that came up for me living in ———— where I lived, and when I went to Dachau, and I couldn't go through Dachau, and actually recollections that are as vivid or more vivid than earlier memories of the sexual molestation, of dying in Dachau, and being a part of that and witnessing sexual abuse, experimentation, and that whole relationship that I had with men in uniform and being sexually abused. . . . My guess is that from this lifetime those sort of memories would have come from my father doing those things to us when we were both very young.

Another survivor, forty years of age, also identified with the Holocaust as her fear of the perpetrator became merged with the fears of antisemitism and Nazism that pervaded the Jewish community in which she was raised:

My childhood fears were connected to the Nazis. I was very scared of the German language which sounds a lot like Yiddish and that was a language that the perpetrator spoke. I was scared of the Nazi soldiers in the war movies and I felt very identified with the concentration camp victims. Throughout my childhood, dinner table

37

conversation was often about the war and the horror of the camps and so I projected all of my fears onto the Nazis who were safer to fear than the real danger in my life, a man who everyone idolized and who was feared by everyone in the family. Only later, while recovering in therapy, did I make the connection between the rape trauma that I repressed and the fears of the Nazis that were so strong in my childhood.

While these two examples of repression and distortion focus on the internalization of Nazi symbols of atrocity and sadism by victimized children, the more common representations of inter-nalized fear are those that are associated with images of spiritual evil and supernatural demons. Among the survivors in this study, nearly half the respondents exhibited symptoms of post traumat-ic stress disorder in which religious symbols of evil were internalized as representations of the abuser, suggesting that the trauma of incest may result in the "demonization" of the perpe-trator.[8] Respondents who manifested this adaptive response were from a variety of religious and ethnic backgrounds, including Latina Catholic, white Presbyterian, black Evangelical, and Pentecostal Protestant. Three examples drawn from the accounts of the survivors help to illustrate the way in which religious cul-ture affects the process of distortion and idealization.

The first example is that of a seventeen-year-old Latina respondent who described the extent to which belief in the spirit world informed the family culture in which she was raised, a blending of indigenous belief systems with European Catholicism. During her interview she described the numerous ways in which evil spirits plagued family members, causing death in infants and interfering in the love relations between men and women. Among the stories she related was that of her aunt who encoun-tered the devil at a dance in Mexico:

> She walked in with her boyfriend, my uncle now, and she said they were dancing and a real handsome guy walked over to her on the

dance floor. He asked her for a slow dance and it was around two o'clock in the morning. She looked down and she noticed that his feet were like goat feet. She was scared. She turned around for a minute and when she turned back he was gone.

This story is a variation of the mythology surrounding La Llorona, the religious symbol of the suffering female sinner.[9] As this young respondent described a childhood in which she was abused both by her father and her uncle, she reconstructed her fear of violation through the belief system that had been accountable for much of the pain and suffering endured by other family members. Here she recounts a memory from early childhood in which she feared the intrusion of a demon spirit:

Where we were sleeping, I was far from my mom's bedroom because she was on the other side of the house. Then I heard it and I was praying, please go away. It was so scary as it came towards my door. I couldn't even scream. Nothing would come out. . . . I get dreams like somebody is standing there and watching me, or somebody or something is going to fool with the bed. Mostly it feels like there's a spirit there, something evil and it just scares me.

For other young women the feared spiritual intruder took residence in dolls whose eyes glowed in the dark and frightened the sleeping child, or, as in the case of a fifteen-year-old respondent raised in the black church, the devil entered her room through a night light:

I had a dream that I saw the devil. I just woke up and there was this guy with a pointed beard sort of like my father. I had a Donald Duck light and it glowed red. I looked up from my red light and there was the devil coming toward me with this red glowing.

One final example of this phenomenon is provided by a white, twenty-one-year-old survivor who was raised according to the teachings of the Presbyterian Church. Her retrospective account of childhood captures the way in which demonology intersects with Christianity to create a social construction of victimization which helps sustain the ideal of the good father:

> I think I viewed my body with shame and hated my body and that fit with Christianity and I believed that the devil had been directly involved in my life. . . . I remember lying in bed at night, especially during the abuse, and I'd lie like this because I always had this image of this hand, claws coming up onto the bed like this, and that it was a demon. Definitely the devil under my bed. I peeked over and there would be this ghoulish thing with horns under my bed so it was definitely involved in my private life in the bedroom which is also the place where I was abused. I was terrified of the claw and I always knew that the devil was real.

As this respondent spoke of her fantasy life, she recognized the similarity between the perpetrator and the demonic images that plagued her imagination:

> The demons were always male, never female. And they had big hands. I think that definitely ties in with my dad. Really big hands, and knobby knuckles, warts, disfigurement, and real bushy eyebrows. My father also has bushy eyebrows—and then bulging eyes and fangs. They were always like a man, a man like my father who appeared grotesque and distorted.

Here again the victimized daughter reconstructs the danger in her life through images of evil and terror that shield her from the true identity of the abuser. The psychiatrist Catherine Schieve has described this phenomenon as a "reversion to magic" among abused children whose belief in the supernatural is a creative and imaginative response to victimization.[10]

It is significant to note that the demonization of the incest perpetrator, as described here by respondents, is reminiscent of descriptions of the devil found in the witchcraft confessions of the sixteenth and seventeenth centuries. Reading these confessions, one is reminded of the screen memories reported by the respondents. For example, H. R. Trever Roper discusses the confession of Francoise Fontaine, a young peasant girl in France who spoke of the devil entering her room at night, of his cold touch, and her own helplessness against his assaults.[11] This confession, given voluntarily without threat or torture, contains many of the elements of spirituality, evil, fear, and violence that are found in the reports of contemporary survivors. Further, the witchcraft confessions, like the present day accounts of incest, are also reminiscent of the case studies of hysteria reported by Freud,[12] an observation that Freud himself recorded in a now-famous letter to his colleague, Wilhelm Fliess:

> By the way, what have you got to say to the suggestion that the whole of my brand-new theory of the primary origins of hysteria is already familiar and has been published a hundred times over, though several centuries ago? Do you remember my always saying that the medieval theory of possession, that held by the ecclesiastical courts, was identical with our theory of a foreign body and the splitting of consciousness? But why did the devil who took possession of the poor victims invariably commit misconduct with them, and in such horrible ways? Why were the confessions extracted under torture so very like what my patients tell me under psychological treatment?[13]

Judith Herman maintains that the answer to Freud's question is found in the "disguised language" of the supernatural which masks the terrifying truth of sexual abuse.[14] Similarly, Jeffrey Masson, in his critique of Freud's suppression of the seduction theory, contends that reports of the supernatural can be understood as the distorted imaging of a trauma that is too painful and horrific to be recorded accurately in memory.[15]

That the spiritual realm becomes the lens through which the daughter filters the trauma of sexual abuse may in part be explained through a Freudian interpretation of God and the unconscious. According to Freud, the symbols of God and Satan are unconscious projections of the real father:

> The contradictions in the original nature of God are, however, a reflection of the ambivalence which governs the relation of the individual to his [her] personal father. If the benevolent and right-eous God is a substitute for his [her] father, it is not to be wondered at that the hostile attitude to his [her] father, too, which is one of hating and fearing him and of making complaints against him, should have come to expression in the creation of Satan. Thus, the father, it seems, is the individual prototype of both God and the Devil.[16]

For abused children in particular, and especially those raised in religious households, this symbol system provides a receptive framework in which to interpret and give meaning to their victimization, as repressed fear and hatred of the perpetrator take form in the images of evil defined by religious culture. The demonization of the perpetrator can therefore be understood as the splitting off of god the father from god the devil, as the former retains the quality of idealization and the latter is attributed with the violence and shame of abuse. These distortions, which protect the child from an intolerable reality, are reinforced by the cultural denial of incest and the attendant idealization of the father in patriarchal society. As a result, the victim's fears and terrors are mislabeled as either the true work of the devil or the psychosis of disturbed women.

Self-Blame and the Idealization of the Father

While repression and distortion represent one adaptation to traumatic sexualization, self-blame provides another cognitive framework through which cultural belief systems surrounding good and evil contribute to maintaining the ideal of the benevolent father. The research on self-blame among incest survivors suggests that in assuming responsibility for the abuse, the victimized daughter internalizes an innate sense of her own evil nature, a response that in part may be attributed to stages of child development that are normally characterized by a certain egocentricity.[17] Thus, as Karin Meiselman points out, children will ordinarily believe they are responsible for divorce or other hurtful situations that befall their family or themselves.[18] Such beliefs contribute to a sense of needed security under conditions of traumatic sexualization, as Elaine Carmen and Patricia Rieker explain:

> Victims of physical and sexual abuse are faced with a formidable and complex series of social, emotional, and cognitive tasks in trying to make sense of experiences that threaten bodily integrity and life itself. Confrontations with violence challenge one's basic assumptions about the self as invulnerable and intrinsically worthy, and about the world as orderly and just. After abuse, the victim's view of self and world can never be the same again. It must be reconstructed to incorporate the abuse experience. In an effort to reduce the inevitable feelings of helplessness and vulnerability, victims frequently tend to assume responsibility for the abuse, thereby restoring an illusion of control.[19]

The sense of false security that is derived from feelings of self-blame ultimately contribute to the development of the "bad" or evil self, a distortion, which like the demonization of incest, is reinforced by cultural and religious belief systems that depict women as sexually corrupt and licentious. Judith Herman has documented the tendency for victimized daughters to identify with sinful and immoral women, frequently labeling themselves as prostitutes and whores.[20] According to Christine Courtois, this aspect of negative identity formation originates out of the contradictions which sexual abuse poses for the child as she seeks to accommodate the reality of sexual violation. She thus concludes:

> The contradiction between what the parent (or other perpetrator) *is* and what he *is supposed to be* is too great for the child to reconcile. She copes with this contradiction as best she can, usually by reversing it. She sees the perpetrator as good in order to protect herself from the disillusionment that would result if she were to view him as bad. She sees *herself* as the bad one who somehow provoked the behavior.[21]

In the mind of the child, incest thus becomes an act of complicity for which she holds herself responsible, an adaptation that may further separate her from her mother against whom, in the family, the "sin" is also committed. The following account of a twenty-one-year-old, white, middle-class survivor powerfully illustrates this effect of sexual violence on the daughter:

> The most traumatic memory for me happened while we were moving. We had to stay in a hotel room. My dad decided that I would sleep with my brother and we were like no, we hate each other. He would hit me and I would scream and so they separated us. But instead of me sleeping with my Mom, my Dad made me sleep with him and that's how it was for the whole trip. The beds were like very close together, and he abused me while cuddling up behind me and just molesting me and then I remember forcibly—this one thing I hang on to—I did move away from him. I tried to move away, but the whole time my Mom's face was right there and she was asleep and I was just looking at her face while he did this to me. . . . She was asleep the whole time, but I was fearful that she would wake up because by then I began to think it was something my father and I were doing together, and I would be caught and in trouble when she woke up and saw me. After that night, I said I'll sleep on the floor. I was twelve years old.

In this poignant recollection, the young daughter may unconsciously wish that her mother would awaken and save her. Consciously, however, she anxiously fears that if she is "caught," she, rather than the perpetrator, will be punished. This social construction of the victimizing dynamic is undoubtedly influenced by the mother's idealization of the father as well, as the child's fantasy of the good and loving parent is informed by the mother's fantasy of the good and loving husband in the abusive family. The child therefore comes to see herself as the offending daughter while the image of the ideal father is preserved.

The interpretive framework that the child brings to this understanding of her victimization reflects ideologies that depict women as evil and sexually promiscuous, as the child identifies with those cultural and religious symbols that portray women as seductive and sinful. Although the vast majority of the women in this study internalized this form of negative identity formation, those respondents raised within religious families were especially likely to identify with symbols of destructive female sexuality. The following excerpt from a Catholic survivor's written recollection of her childhood will help to illustrate this point:

> I want to tell you about being seven
> about growing through seven in the shadow of the Church
> in the shadow of living shadows—nuns in long black dresses
> whispering litanies sins. . . .
> The only official word for sex in the Church: adultery
> in the Ten Commandments
> in our Holy Catechism
> in the mouths of the nuns
> I was Lolita
> Adulterer, Lillith in my seven year old mind. . . .[22]

Another Catholic survivor, now twenty-two years old, also spoke of her identification with the image of the prostitute:

> I always thought I was bad because of what I was doing with him. They would have stories in church about sinners like Mary Magdalene. Prostitute was the word they used. That's what I thought I was at 11 years old, a slut who was a sinner.

The virgin/whore dichotomy which informs the self concept of incest survivors takes on racial and ethnic connotations as well. Among Latina respondents the internalization of the female sinner reflects the symbol systems of colonial oppression.[23] Identifying with cultural and religious representations of *La Chingada*, the raped mother, or *La Llorona*, the suffering sinner, the victimized Latina child sees herself in the image of the *puta*, the prostitute, who both suffers and is abandoned for her sinfulness.[24] Cherrie Moraga, writing in *Loving in the War Years*, describes the way in which Latina women internalize the image of Malinche, the guide and mistress of Cortez who, in her association with *La Chingada*, is a powerful symbol of female sin and betrayal:

> Coming from such a complex and contradictory history of sexual exploitation by white men and from within our own race, it is nearly earth shaking to begin to try and separate the myths told about us from the truths; and to examine to what extent we have internalized what, in fact, is not true.
>
> Although intellectually I knew different, early-on I learned that women were the willing cooperators in rape. So over and over again in pictures, books, movies, I experienced rape and pseudo-rape as titillating, sexy, as what sex was all about. Women want it. . . .
>
> I learned these notions about sexuality not only from the society at large, but more specifically and potently from Chicano/Mexicano culture, originating from the myth of La Chingada, Malinche. In the very act of intercourse with Cortez, Malinche is seen as having been violated. She is not, however, an innocent victim, but the guilty party—ultimately responsible for her own sexual victimization.[25]

In the African American community, such racist legacies, which define women of color as the sexually objectified other, originate out of the sexual violence of slavery in which black women were portrayed as sexual and animalistic.[26] In this regard, Patricia Hill Collins discusses the effect of racism on violence against women in the black community:

Rape and other acts of overt violence that Black women have experienced, such as physical assault during slavery, domestic abuse, incest, and sexual extortion, accompany Black women's subordination in a system of race, class, and gender oppression. . . . Specific acts of sexual violence visited on African-American women reflect a broader process by which violence is socially constructed in a race- and gender-specific manner. . . . Treating African-American women as pornographic objects and portraying them as sexualized animals, as prostitutes, created the controlling image of the Jezebel. Rape became the specific act of sexual violence forced on Black women, with the myth of the Black prostitute as its ideological justification.[27]

For the victimized daughter, these racially stigmatizing myths assume a painful dimension of reality as these images are internalized both by the abuser and the victim. Incest thus reinforces a female identity of prostitute and sinful child that is linked to racial oppression. An African American teen mother, seventeen years of age, described the way in which this evil persona was reinforced by her role as the "bad one" in the family:

When I was growing up I got a lot of attention because I was the bad one, the really bad one. My mom said, "every time we woke up we were scared to wake up, because you were always a challenge." She said, "yes, you were very bad." She says that's okay because it will come back on you because that little one, the baby, she's going to get you.

In addition, the race and gender stereotyping which stigmatizes African American women has a corollary in the historical depiction of the hypersexual black male.[28] This myth too impacts the black incest survivor whose victimization is treated with less serious concern by social service agencies that attribute sexual abuse in black communities to race-specific behaviors associated with promiscuous girls and sexually unrestrained men.[29] In their research on treatment of incest among African Americans,

Carolyn Thornton and James Carter discuss the racial stereotyping that is pervasive in both the scientific community and the legal system:

> The omission of incest among blacks in scientific literature may be related to the many myths and misconceptions about black family interactions and psychopathology. Folklore and research depict the black man as preoccupied with his role as sexual partner; the concept of black male hypersexuality dates back as far as the 16th century, when Englishmen described Africans as beset by an unrestrained lustfulness. . . . Thus, the sexual life of a black person may not be judged by the moral standards of the larger society, and therein lies the problem. From their experience, the authors contend that society does not hold sexual misconduct among blacks to be of an equal degree of magnitude, as evidenced by the scarcity of law enforcement involvement in the reported cases of black incest described in this paper. Rather, when incest is reported in black families, it is often minimized or disregarded by agencies assigned to investigate and treat the problem.[30]

The effect of such negligence is that victimized children remain at risk, while the self-blame of the daughter is reinforced by a form of cultural oppression that fails to identify or take action against the wrongful behavior of the perpetrator.

As this analysis suggests, victimized daughters from diverse racial and ethnic backgrounds internalize religious and cultural belief systems in such a way as to reinforce their culpability for the abusive relationship. Further, as the perpetrator frequently blames the child for his sexual violence, the internalization of misogynistic images of female sexuality is informed by the shame and self-hatred of the abuser. As such, Louise Wisechild offers this memory of oral rape by her incestuous grandfather, a religious authoritarian who, after the death of her father, assumed the role of paternal parent:

> My grandfather's hands are very big and scratchy. He doesn't put lotion on them like Grandma. When he puts his hands on my

shoulders they cover my arms and his hands pull me toward his candy. But it doesn't smell good, it smells like the bathroom. "Open your mouth," he says, and his voice is tight like a piece of twine. He moves my arms around his legs, they are bigger than tree trunks and my fists hold on because everything is swimming and I'm going to fall down soon.

"Put it in your mouth," he says, "suck it." It tastes like raw sausages. My tongue curls inside of my mouth. I try to pull away but his hands are cupped around the back of my head. . . .

"You're a bad girl for making Grandpa do this," Grandpa had said. His voice sounded different, frantic, gruff. I knew that what was happening was bad.[31]

Other survivors similarly reported that the perpetrator referred to them as sluts and whores, constructing an identity of the sinful woman which justified the violation of the daughter. The religious and cultural denigration of women thus provides the basis upon which the perpetrator legitimates his violence while the daughter internalizes cultural representations of her evil and wanton nature. In one such case, a young woman described the feelings she experienced during the rapes by her stepfather, a religious man, active in the black church, who justified his incestuous assaults with references to the Bible:

The only thing going through my head was why is he doing this? The whole time, I kept thinking, why is he doing this to me? And I'd get upset at myself and I'd think, what did I do to make him do this?

In the case cited above, the survivor responded to her stepfather's biblical pronouncements with both skepticism and feelings of fear that God might in fact condone the rape of a child:

My mom and him were into church real big. He started talking about stuff, like God gave him everything and stuff out of the Bible. He said he had to teach me about sex and everything. I've always questioned it but he read some scripture out of the Bible. It scared me that he was talking to me about this, like he was God. He just scared me.

In an important crosscultural study of Christianity and incest in the Netherlands, Ineke Jonker, a historian and incest survivor, described her experience of religious denigration within the context of white European culture:

Since I began talking about my own sexual abuse with other abused women from the Association against Child Abuse within the Family in 1982, it has gradually become clearer to me that I am not only tormented about the abuse itself, but also about my religious feelings which were violated in a brutal and systematic way. For years, my mother's father, who was also my rapist, regularly told me that women are unclean, evil, sinners, sly, and devious creatures who are constantly trying to rob men of their strength. These "lessons" were illustrated with stories from the Bible: Potiphar's wife, Issac's wife, Samson's wife, not to mention Eve.[32]

Religious and cultural validation for the abuse, combined with the violation of the child, has detrimental consequences for the personality formation of the daughter who comes to perceive herself as truly evil and seductively powerful. Herman explains this effect of incest as follows:

The child entrapped in this kind of horror develops the belief that she is somehow responsible for the crimes of her abusers. Simply by virtue of her existence on earth, she believes that she has driven the most powerful people in her world to do terrible things. Surely, then, her nature must be thoroughly evil. The language of the self becomes a language of abomination. . . .

By developing a contaminated, stigmatized identity, the child victim takes the evil of the abuser into herself and thereby preserves her primary attachments to her parents. Because the inner sense of badness preserves a relationship, it is not readily given up even after the abuse has stopped; rather, it becomes part of the child's personality structure.[33]

The attachment to the perpetrator and to his idealized persona is thus maintained through the internalization of the evil self who inhabits the interior world of the child. This identification with evil and malevolence is expressed by a white, twenty-one-year-old respondent who described the fear of evil within herself:

> It's always been inside my head that I have the capacity to do really evil things. . . . For instance, like looking over a railing and you feel you could jump and there is a voice inside your head saying, "Jump." Or babysitting, thinking I could do something to those children, and a voice inside my head saying, "I could just take a knife" and really visualizing it. It really scares me to think of what is inside of me, like there's another wicked person inside of me, like little flashes of another me.

The notion that a truly evil "other" is embedded deep within the victimized daughter is a reflection of the sexual nature of her violation. The penetration of her body is experienced as the penetration of her true self, creating within her psychic being a place of evil and shame that is a source of stigma and self hatred. For some survivors, this negative identity formation results in their entry into prostitution. Ellen Pillard, among others,[34] has studied the correlation between childhood sexual abuse and prostitution. Based on her research, she concludes that:

> The "good girl" image is either unrealistic, unattainable or nonexistent. The only, or at least the most significant attention the female child receives is around her sexuality. . . . Usually this linking of sex with attention and value comes after sexuality is identified with the "bad girl" image. With these dynamics the young girl gets repeated messages that she is "bad" because she is sexual and yet the only attention or value she receives is around her sexuality . . . it is these events in association with the absence

of a positive healthy sense of self and the existence of arbitrary and absolute constructions of "good girl" and "bad girl" roles that predispose women to enter prostitution.[35]

Two young women in this study, a white adolescent, seventeen years of age, and a nineteen-year-old, African American survivor, had, as Pillard descibes, entered prostitution soon after reaching puberty. The majority of respondents, however, rather than turn toward this resolution of the bad self, developed an idealized persona to overcome the evil and seductive child within. Herman has called this adaptation to abuse the development of the "double self,"[36] a personality construct which is found among those survivors who repress the victimization as well as those who cope consciously with the ongoing violence in their lives. Accordingly, there are many ways in which the idealized self may be expressed, as the high achieving student, the socially successful adolescent, or the talented and creative daughter, identities which seek to undermine the true sense of self-hatred that informs the development of the violated child. In the families where strong religious values prevail, the idealized self may be constructed in the image of the saintly child. A twenty-three-year-old, white, working-class survivor describes her achievement in a Fundamentalist church:

> I grew up in the church and was really very involved. I was a missionette which is like girl scouts. I was an honor star and I got a scholarhsip to an Assemblies of God college. When you go to the missionette retreat, you take this test and I got all the answers right and I got to wear a crown and I was on the quiz team. I memorized the whole book of Romans, word for word. I knew every word of Romans, Book One and Two, sixteen chapters, and I was the highest quizzer in the state when I was in seventh grade.

Other survivors developed the ideal self in a more secularized context, excelling in academics, sports, or the arts. A white, thirty-two-year-old respondent from a middle-class background assumed the role of performer early in her life:

> My image of myself as a little kid was that I was funny, entertaining, and very talented. I was doing piano lessons and voice lessons and theater and I was performing a lot. . . . I remember when I sang I thought people are probably surprised that such a beautiful voice comes out of such an ugly person. I deeply felt that I was ugly, unworthy, shameful. So I sang and danced and everything to look better.

A significant influence in the construction of the idealized self is the extent to which the daughter's alternative identity is informed by the idealization of the perpetrator and the attending empathic connection that develops between victim and abuser, an attachment which underlies the self-in-relation that comes to characterize the personality of the violated daughter.

4

⤸

Sexual Violence and the Empathic Female Self

Soul Murder is neither a diagnosis nor a condition. It is a dramatic term for a circumstance that eventuates in crime—the deliberate attempt to eradicate or compromise the separate identity of another person. The victims of soul murder remain in large part possessed by another, their souls in bondage to someone else.

—Leonard Shengold

Much of the recent scholarship on the development of the female self has focused on the importance of relationality as a defining characteristic of the feminine personality,[1] that quality of femaleness which distinguishes men from women in all aspects of human endeavor, including parenting, intimacy, moral judgment, and scientific inquiry.[2] In contrast to the male-centered interpretations of human personality that focus primarily on autonomy and separateness, the relational model of development emphasizes the significance of attachment for women and the value of the relational self.[3] Within this paradigm, the importance of empathy has been stressed as "the process through which one's experienced sense of basic connection and similarity to other humans is established."[4]

In constructing theoretical models of empathic connection, the mother-daughter relationship has been the developmental model through which feminist scholars have sought to explain the child's ability to experience the inner state of another. Writing on self-in-relation theory, Janet Surrey describes the significance of the mother-daughter relationship:

> The ability of the mother to listen and respond, empathize or "mirror" the child's feelings has been well described by Winnicott (1971), Kohut (1971), and others; it has also been seen as the beginning of the development of the experience of the self. Here we are describing the girl's open relationship with the mother and the mother's open relationship with the daughter as the beginning stage for the development of self-in-relation.[5]

This understanding of the female relational self is predicated on the presence of a mutually empathic bond between mother and child that contributes to the healthy psychosocial development of the daughter. When, however, the child's empathic development is contextualized by the father's sexual abuse, a rupture in the mother-daughter bond takes place such that victimized daughters, as described in the previous chapter, tend to empathize with and forgive fathers while turning their anger and rage toward their mothers. Thus, empathic development emerges through the attachment to the perpetrator who exploits both the emotional and physical boundaries of the female child. Through an exploration of the phenomenon of empathic bonding between victim and perpetrator, this chapter offers a perspective on the relationship among sexual violence, cultural norms of male entitlement,[6] and the distortions that come to characterize the development of the empathic female self. As such, this analysis expands the mother-centered model of self-in-relation by examining the impact of paternal violence on the personality of the female child.

The Self-in-Relation and the Social Construction
of Empathy

As a component of the female personality, empathy is often described as the ability to feel what others feel, to experience the emotional state of the other such that one becomes sensitive to and responsive to the other's needs.[7] Accordingly, Judith Jordan writes that

> Experientially, empathy begins with some general motivation for interpersonal relatedness that allows the perception of the other's affective cues (both verbal and nonverbal) followed by surrender to affective arousal in oneself. This involves temporary identification with the other's state, during which one is aware that the source of the affect is in the other.[8]

Studies of ego development suggest that the empathic self develops out of the child's identification with a significant other to whom she or he feels deep attachment and connection. In the traditional psychoanalytic literature, the source of empathic response is found in the experience of merging, an infantile connectedness in which the child experiences her/himself as one with the primary source of love and nurturing.[9] Over the last decade, feminist scholarship, objecting to the regressive connotations in such interpretations, has reframed the phenomenon of merging within the context of social interaction. The self-in-relation theorists suggest that empathy, rather than a manifestation of merged identity, originates out of the interactive dynamic between caregiver and child. Jean Baker Miller concludes:

> the infant, actively exerting an effect on the relationship, begins to develop an internal sense of itself as one who changes the emotional interplay for both participants. . . . Part of this internal image of oneself includes feeling the other's emotions and *acting on* them as they are in interplay with one's own emotions.[10]

It is thus the exchange of feeling and emotion between social actors which provides the foundation for the development of an empathic personality, the relational self that, because of the gendered nature of child rearing, becomes associated with the feminine persona. That empathy becomes gendered in Western culture is, according to this view, a consequence primarily of patriarchal family structure. As daughters are nurtured principally by women, they develop fluid ego boundaries that allow for the interplay of emotion that forms the basis for empathic responsiveness. Such an understanding of female development, most closely associated with the work of Nancy Chodorow and Dorothy Dinnerstein, focuses exclusively on the significance of mothering in the formation of the female personality.[11] Within this paradigm, Surrey describes the mother's role specifically in relation to the development of female empathy:

> The mother's easier emotional openness with the daughter than with the son, along with her sense of identification with this style of personal learning and exploration, probably leave the daughter feeling more emotionally connected, understood, and recognized. This sense of connection forms the framework necessary for the process of differentiation and clarification that will follow. The key factor here is the idea that the mutual sharing process fosters a sense of mutual understanding and connection.[12]

In comparison with the mother-centered model of development, the role of the father has been studied much less extensively and generally has been considered of lesser importance. The scholarly literature on fathers and daughters offers two somewhat conflicting interpretations of the significance of fathering to personality formation. The psychological approach favored by theorists such as Shulamith Firestone and Jessica Benjamin stress the value of the father as a symbol of autonomy through which the process of individuation is facilitated.[13] This view holds that the father represents an independent form of attachment in contrast to the symbiotic ties represented by the mother; it is through this relationship that the daughter becomes individuated.[14] Studies of sex role socialization, on the other hand, suggest that fathers sex type to a much greater extent than mothers, socializing their daughters toward "femininity" and the roles of nurturer and caretaker.[15] As early as the 1950s, crosscultural studies of sex differences in socialization explored the way in which nurturance and obedience become part of the cultural world of female children, as girls are pressured toward caretaking and compliance while boys are directed toward achievement and self reliance.[16] Later studies have confirmed these findings, emphasizing in particular the role that fathers assume with regard to the "feminization" of daughters.[17] Michele Wallace writes of her stepfather's socializing influence within an African American family where strong female role models prevailed:

> I can't remember when I first learned that my family expected me to work, to be able to take care of myself when I grew up. My mother was so extraordinarily career-oriented that I was never allowed to take lessons in anything unless I manifested a deep interest in a career in that area. . . .
>
> The fact that my family expected me to work and have a career should have made the things I wanted very different from what little white girls wanted according to the popular sociological view. But I don't believe any sociologist took into account a man like my stepfather. My stepfather gave me "housewife lessons." It was he who taught me how to clean house and how I should act around men. "Don't be like your mother," he told me. "She's a nice lady but she's a bad wife. She was lucky with me. I want you to get a *good* husband."
>
> . . . Growing up in Harlem, I listened to these messages no less intently than the little white girls who grew up on Park Avenue, in Scarsdale, and on Long Island. In a way I needed to hear them, to believe them, even more than they did.[18]

Such observations on female development suggest that the social construction of the female self emerges out of a complex interactive framework of social relations that involve fathers as well as mothers and is contextualized by the cultural norms of male entitlement. Thus, as Marcia Westkott points out, theories of female personality development must take into account the presence of fathers in the psychodynamics of the family, a presence which is characterized by the demand for nurturance and caretaking.[19] Families in which sexual violence predominates represent the most extreme form of social learning in which the female child comes to experience herself through the emotional and physical demands of the father/perpetrator. Westkott offers this perspective on the violated daughter's relationship to the incestuous father:

> At the same time, the daughter is in her very powerlessness accessible to him; in her dependence upon him, she cannot refuse him; and in her naive but defensive "love" of him, she gives him the unconditional love and validation he craves. He is both the uncontested and dominant sexual predator and the eternally beloved and cared-for son.[20]

Within the incestuous family, it is the father who controls the emotional exchange between child and parent through which relationality is both learned and reinforced. Empathic responsiveness is therefore structured around nurturing and care of the perpetrator. Under conditions of sexual violence, the needs of the father are at the center of the daughter's emotional life, as he imposes his will and his emotional demands onto the victimized child.

As such, the multiple boundary violations which inform the child's relationship to the perpetrator create a dynamic of forced intimacy wherein attachment rather than separateness defines the daughter's relationship to the father. The forced intimacy characteristic of incest perpetration acts to separate the daughter from her mother, reinforcing the child's feelings of maternal betrayal and abandonment while intensifying her connection to the abusive parent. The accounts of survivors in this study suggest that forced intimacy is experienced by the abused child in a number of different contexts that characterize incest families. While there is a wide range of experiences which speak to this aspect of victimization, the data from the sexual abuse literature and from the retrospective life histories suggest that incestuous fathers contextualize the abuse by linking shame, self pity, and emotional demands to the act of sexual violence. Each of these dimensions of forced intimacy will be explored in relation to the social construction of female empathy.

Violence and Remorse

Perhaps the clearest expression of the interrelationship between physical and emotional boundary violations occurs when sexual abuse becomes most violent. It is then that survivors recount the terror of rape, the pain of violation, and the confusion which surrounds an act of aggression for which the young victim has no name. For over half the women in this study, violated before the age of eight, the concept of sexual assault was not understood until many years after the violence had occurred, when the survivor had the language and the conceptual framework to recognize and acknowledge the unnamed trauma of her early childhood.

While it is often difficult and sometimes impossible to give words to this experience, Maya Angelou in her autobiography poignantly recounts her rape by the man she had fantasized as a loving father. Here she describes how the desire to be nurtured becomes the prelude to a violent assault:

> I didn't want to admit that I had in fact liked his holding me or that I had liked his smell or the hard heart-beating, so I said nothing. . . .

61

Then there was the pain. A breaking and entering when even the senses are torn apart. The act of rape on an eight-year-old body is a matter of the needle giving because the camel can't. The child gives, because the body can, and the mind of the violator cannot.

I thought I had died—I woke up in a white-walled world, and it had to be heaven. But Mr. Freeman was there and he was washing me. His hands shook, but he held me upright in the tub and washed my legs. "I didn't mean to hurt you, Ritie. I didn't mean it. But don't you tell . . . Remember, don't you tell a soul."[21]

In this retelling of the rape, Angelou reconstructs the child self who simultaneously experiences the suffering of the victim while responding to the remorse of the victimizer. Immediately after the assault, the perpetrator is caring for her and apologizing, asking that she, the abused child, understand that he did not mean to hurt her. And she in turn is aware of his shaking hands even while her own body feels shattered and torn. In that moment of awareness, the physical and emotional boundary violations converge as the child feels both her pain and the pain of the abuser. Empathy is thus engendered under conditions of sexual violence, resulting in the development of an empathic bond in which the feelings of the perpetrator take precedence, displacing the child's emotional connection to the violated self. The following written account of an adult survivor offers further insight into the way in which the focus of pain shifts from the abused to the abuser, as the remorse of the perpetrator defines the context under which sexual aggression takes place:

I see me, four years old. Thin blondish hair. Little girl face. White pajamas with little blue flowers. My father is crying and telling me to be good. He pulls down my pajama bottoms and tries to put something too big inside my vagina . . . I am terrified that my father is crying. I won't mind the hurt if it will make him stop crying. The big thing won't go in, though, and he is still crying. He stops and tells me I must love him. I lie still and he puts that big thing into my mouth. He is holding my nose. I can't breathe. He won't stop and I feel guilty for fighting it. He needs me.[22]

As this account makes painfully aware, the emotions of the perpetrator bring forth nurturing and sympathy from the daughter who wishes to alleviate the suffering of her father. Through his demands for love and compliance, the perpetrator violates the core of the child's emotional being as his gratification informs the experience of the victimized child who cannot yet distinguish between her own desire for safety and love and the needs of the incestuous father. Brendan MacCarthy explains:

> The young child's total passive compliance, as a response to father's overwhelming need, is the only course for the child, at any rate if she loves her father. She knows he needs this experience, although she may not know why.[23]

As attachment is fostered through violence, the child responds by empathizing with the abuser who at once deprives her of her right to bodily integrity and emotional autonomy. One final illustration of this form of forced intimacy is evident in the account of a thirty-five-year-old survivor from a white, middle-class background who had been raped before the age of five. As she reconstructed the trauma of the assault many years later, this woman, like Maya Angelou, thought that such a form of violence could only mean death. Here she recounts the memory of the experience:

> I opened my eyes and I saw a bright light through the window. I realized I had not died, that I was still alive. There at the end of the table where I had been tied I saw him crying. His face was all red and there were tears streaming down his face. At that moment I felt sorry for him. He was sobbing and I knew it was somehow my fault. I must have done something terrible to make him do what he did to me and then to make him cry.

During this act of violation, the child victim not only recognizes the primacy of the aggressor's pain but takes responsibility both for the rape and for his remorse. Here, as in the other two cases cited above, the child experiences the perpetrator's violent behavior in connection with his guilt and shame. It is thus his shame which she comes to identify as her own. Unable to understand the meaning of the sexual behavior, the young victim nonetheless understands that it is shameful and wrong as secrecy and compliance are demanded of the violated daughter. The following excerpt from a narrative written by a survivor illustrates the way in which empathy infused with shame underlies the identity formation of the abused child:

> I go to the garage to get my bike and he is there, working in his lighted corner. I know I am trapped.
>
> "Honey, come back here a minute."
>
> I slide between him and the car fender and when he asks I lift my T-shirt. He touches them and I smile when he looks at my face. I must show him it is all right with me. But I don't like it. They are larger and more embarrassing, cold puckering the skin around the nipples. He is funny, breathless and giggly, different from his usual stern self. But it's not hurting me, and if I object, it will hurt him. He would see that I know it is wrong. I couldn't bear for him to think that.[24]

Through her empathic attachment to the perpetrator, the daughter assumes responsibility for his feelings which contribute to her own confusion over the initiation of sexual violence. Such boundary confusion further reinforces the self-blame and guilt of the child, particularly as the self pity of the perpetrator defines the emotional climate around which the incest occurs.

The "Victimized" Perpetrator

Male entitlement in incest families often assumes a quality of pathos as abusive and violent fathers portray themselves as victims within the family. Compliance is engendered through an appeal to the empathic female child who feels both fear and sympathy for the perpetrator. As one daughter of working-class parents described this family dynamic:

> My father would always make me feel sorry for him. He had a way about him that said, "Poor little me." He would say things like, "Nobody gives a shit about me, they just care if my paycheck comes in." When he would say things like that I would always feel sorry for him. One day I remember yelling at him and he gave me the silent treatment and wouldn't talk to me. I gave him this little note. I wrote, "Dad, I'm really sorry." The next morning he came up to my bedroom and I remember him kissing me.

As expressed by this respondent, the violation of the daughter is carried out through a context of victimization in which the father exploits the emotional vulnerability of the child as her empathy and concern for him become the basis for sexual exploitation. This form of coercion is most evident among those abusive fathers who, through forced intimacy, forge a victim-perpetrator alliance, constructing a shared identity with the daughter that isolates her emotionally and psychologically from her mother. One such case involved a white, middle-class survivor who described how her father preferred her company to that of her mother, sharing his interests and feelings with her alone:

> When he came home from work, he would always tell me about his day. He wouldn't tell mom about what was going on. Maybe he thought I would understand better. I felt sorry for him because he always got blamed for everything. When I was home I was the scapegoat. When I wasn't home he was the scapegoat and still is now.

While the daughter's identification with a male parent is not exclusive to victimization,[25] such identification is often fostered by incestuous fathers who blur the child's ego boundaries—a problem of differentiation frequently attributed to the mother-daughter relationship. Chodorow writes:

> the mother daughter relation is the one form of personal identification that, because it results so easily from the normal situation of child development, is liable to be excessive in the direction of allowing no room for separation or difference between mother and daughter.
>
> The situation reinforces itself in circular fashion. A mother, on the one hand, grows up without establishing adequate ego boundaries or a firm sense of self. She tends to experience boundary confusion with her daughter, and does not provide experiences of differentiating ego development for her daughter or encourage the breaking of her daughter's dependence.[26]

Although fathers are rarely described in similar terms, incest is a prevalent form of family violence in which the ego boundaries of the daughter are invaded by the father. Studies of incestuous fathers suggest that while the perpetrator may seek maternal nurturing in the abusive relationship with his daugher,[27] he does so through an identification with the victimized child who he views as an extention of himself.[28] The findings from this study support the conclusion that some incestuous fathers do indeed identify with their daughters in whom they perceive similar personality traits and shared intellectual interests. One father, for example, repeatedly told his daughter that she was just like him, particularly at those moments when she would become angry and enraged at her mother. In reinforcing this type of father-daughter identification, the abuser further alienates the daughter from her mother as they are forced into competing roles in the incestuous family. The result is that the bond between perpetrator and victimized child is strengthened as she perceives her only ally to be the abuser with whom she empathizes and from whom she receives nurturing. Out of such empathic attachment, the abused child seeks refuge with the parent who violates her, a finding confirmed by Judith Herman's research:

> In the special alliance with their fathers, many daughters found the sense of being cared for which they craved, and which they obtained from no other source. The attentions of their fathers offered some compensation for what was lacking in their relations with their mothers. . . . Moreover, their special relationship with their fathers was often perceived as their only source of affection. Under these circumstances, when their fathers chose to demand sexual services, the daughters felt they had absolutely no option but to comply.[29]

Such attachment creates a painful contradiction for the daughter who perceives that her only source of love in the family is found in her relationship to a sexually abusive father who may also be violent and cruel. This attachment is further confounded by the multiple roles that the perpetrator plays in the child's life, as the father who is abusive may at other times be a source of nurturing for the daughter. Here a white, middle-class survivor recalls how her violent father could also be empathic:

> It was the last semester of my senior year. I was constantly doing all these things and I was just really close to breaking down. I remember I was just crying and my Dad came in and was very nice and I think he put his arm around me and said, "You know, you really don't have to do all this." I looked at him and I was shocked. I thought, of course I do. You've got to be kidding. But it was the only expression that someone saw something that I was doing and empathized with me.

Further, Alice Miller suggests that the "interlinking of love and hate" in the personality of the abused child results from her total dependency on a parent who has been exploitive.[30] Unable to express her anger for fear of losing the father, her development is characterized by ambivalence and an association of love with suffering and sacrifice. The ambivalence which surrounds the victimized daughter's relationship to her father is revealed in a dream related by a twenty-nine-year-old survivor:

> I had a dream not long ago. I was talking to my dad and I was pissed at him. I was saying, "I hate you, I can't stand you, let's get out of here." We were on this cliff and I saw him walking down a cliff. He looked really sad and I felt pretty guilty. I said, "I don't care. I hate him." These people came up to me and said, "He's dying." And I thought, "So, why should I care?" Finally, I ran down the cliff and told him I loved him. I don't know. I guess I must at some level. I think I just feel sorry for him.

This form of attachment is further distorted by the effects of forced intimacy as the perpetrator portrays himself as the family member who is in pain and in need of caretaking.[31] The distress of victimization is thus experienced by the child as the distress of the victimizer for whom she feels responsible. As grief and pain inform her awareness of the abusive relationship, the daughter seeks to rescue the father who has betrayed her.

Rescuing the Perpetrator

One manifestation of the empathic female persona is the desire on the part of victimized women to save those men who batter, abuse, and humiliate them. The origins for such self denial can be found in the emotional exploitation that accompanies the sexual abuse of the daughter as the demands of the perpetrator signify his emotional fragility and neediness. Thus, the act of sexual violence becomes the context in which the child may first experience her wish to save her father both from the anxiety that his incestuous behavior engenders and from the anguish he attributes to his victimization in the family. Through this form of exploitation the daughter comes to value herself according to the protection and caretaking that she offers the perpetrator. This pattern of development, wherein a role reversal between child and parent is established in incest families, has been studied primarily in relation to mothers and daughters. The existing literature on incest discusses the domestic roles that daughters frequently assume in the incestuous household, taking responsibility for childcare, cooking, and cleaning.[32] The focus on the daughter's domesticity has tended to obscure the extent to which incestuous fathers also demand emotional caretaking from their daughters. Survivors speak of saving the perpetrator from depression, divorce, unsatisfactory relationships, and the knowledge of their own abusive behavior. In one case, a white woman from a working-class background described the anguish she experienced over the conflict between self-realization and the continued desire to protect her father:

> I know he raped me, but I just can't let it in yet. I know it happened. It is the hardest thing. My dad has been sick and I am not in a position to tell anyone. If I told him it would kill him.

Prior research has reported similar concerns that daughters may express for mothers in incest families, fearing that disclosure would bring unbearable pain and perhaps even death.[33] Yet, the findings of this study suggest that it is often the perpetrator for whom such concern is expressed, as he is the focus of emotional attachment within the family. Here, a white survivor from an upper-class background describes how such emotional control affected her relationship to the perpetrator throughout childhood and into adolescence:

> When I was growing up my father always acted like my mother didn't care for him. If he wanted something done, we [the children] did it. And if we didn't, he would pout. He acted like a martyr. It was the worst thing in the world. He never yelled, but it was the subtle stuff. It was very powerful—this complete disapproval. I'd be

on the floor. . . . When he moved out, after my parents separated, I felt very sorry for my Dad. He couldn't cook and so I went to cook for him. He didn't know how to do the laundry so I would help him do the laundry. He would put on the whole "pity me" act and I bought into it. I hoped that he would see what a wonderful daughter I have been, someone he can talk to, different from my mother. I was so happy when he moved out. I thought it would be great . . . But it was weird because he just wanted me to take care of him and I kept thinking, but I'm the kid, you're supposed to take care of me.

This account illustrates the way in which male entitlement pervades the socio-emotional interactions of incest families; as Herman points out, the fact that the daughter is a child and the perpetrator an adult is immaterial to the incestuous father.[34] In those situations where the perpetrator manifests symptoms of depression or other forms of psychological dysfunction, empathic responses on the part of the daughter may lead to revictimization in adulthood, a pattern commonly found among survivors.[35] In this regard, repondents reported that frequently they found themselves in abusive relationships which replicated the dynamic of empathic responsiveness that characterized their relationship to their fathers. One example is that of a thirty-five-year-old white survivor who repeatedly became involved with men who appeared needy and helpless:

I get into a relationship with men that I want to save and I think it is because I could see my father's pain and although I tried, I could never do anything to alleviate it. And I wanted to be there to comfort him, or to heal, or to help him.

This form of attachment in adult survivors emerges out of what Jordan has termed "faulty empathy,"[36] a personality construct in which the individual's self boundaries are extremely permeable and thus she cannot easily distinguish between her needs and the needs of others. While the powerlessness and sexual boundary violations of incest contribute greatly to a diminished sense of self, the empathic connection further confounds the developing child's sense of separateness as she constructs her identity through the emotional attachment to the perpetrator. Thus, incest survivors may suffer a loss of self that is re-experienced in intimate relationships. This effect of victimization, reported by both lesbian and heterosexual respondents, is illustrated in the following account of a lesbian survivor in recovery:

> I would often enter into relationships with other women who were needy and vulnerable like myself. I would always assume the role of caretaker—connecting love and being loved with recognizing the pain in others and trying to eliminate that pain. My sense of self was so tied into the emotional needs of my partners that my needs became nonexistent.

In addition, the striving for perfection frequently found among incest survivors has often been explained as the creation of an idealized self, which, as discussed in the previous chapter, compensates for the negative identity of the abused child.[37] The construction of the idealized self, however, might also be understood in relation to the empathy the child feels for the abuser, as she seeks to become the perfect daughter whose "goodness" may alleviate his suffering. A thirty-one-year-old respondent from a middle-class background described the connections between her role as the "good girl" and her father's emotional well-being:

> I think I always sensed that my father was very unhappy and lonely, and I identified with his loneliness. I wanted to make life better for him. I wanted to entertain him, to make him happy, to be the good little girl in his life.

The desire to be the ideal child who alleviates the suffering of the father also may be expressed as an unconscious wish to change the violent father into the idealized parent. As a result, the child may internalize cultural myths which offer the promise of transformation. Among a number of the respondents inter-viewed, fairy tales such as "Beauty and the Beast" were especially meaningful stories with which the injured daughter could identi-fy. In one case, this myth clearly informed the construction of an idealized self:

> My favorite fairy tale was "Beauty and the Beast." I wanted to be like Beauty. I thought I could turn the Beast into the lovely, won-derful creature and if I just kept being sweet and nice and loyal, he would become loving and kind.

Another case, that of a twenty-one-year-old white survivor, speaks to the impact of this myth on the developing child's sense of compassion for the perpetrator:

> "Beauty and the Beast" is still a huge favorite of mine. I loved the pictures in the fairy tale book. I remember looking at these and thinking, she was able to love him and have such compassion for him and he was such an ugly monster. I think there was a lot of identification going on with this story.

As empathy and caretaking define the relational quality of the child's emotional life, the meaning of empathic bonding to the developing self may be variously construed. As suggested earlier, the role of nurturer defines the child as "the good girl," a needed affirmation, which helps to mitigate the self condemnation that accompanies sexual abuse. In caring for the perpetrator, the humiliation, fear, and shame associated with victimization are reframed in a loving, caring relationship through which the child perceives herself as the valued daughter. Nurturing the aggressor thus becomes a strategy for constructing a sense of self-worth under conditions of powerlessness. Such empathic responsiveness, according to Miller, grows "out of attempts to find a possibility of acting within connections when the only connections available present impossibilities."[38] A consequence for the daughter is a sustained connection to the perpetrator, but one which creates severe disconnection from the child-self who has been victimized.[39]

Further, and perhaps more significantly, the emphathic bond may serve to nurture the daughter as well. In seeking to alleviate the distress of the abusive parent, with whom she identifies, the child may seek to alleviate her own suffering and in so doing rescue the violated self from the despair of victimization. This aspect of empathic bonding would suggest that incest informs both the inner and outer reality of the child's life within the family, as she discovers her identity through observing and responding to the feelings of the perpetrator. In the cases described here, the violence experienced by the daughter is reflected in the pain and neediness expressed by the violator. This mirroring of reality is perhaps most poignantly illustrated in the account of sexual assault described earlier where at the very moment of violation the child witnesses her father's grief even as he brutalizes her. As such traumatic conditioning occurs at crucial stages in the child's development, the father's emotional behavior and responses provide an interactive framework against which to assess her own feelings of terror, sadness, and betrayal. It is in the image of the father as suffering victim that the child sees her own reflection and thus his salvation becomes linked to her own needs for nurturance and help. Ultimately, the comfort she offers the abuser is the solace she wishes for herself. The empathic attachment between the victimized daughter and her father therefore becomes the emotional framework through which the identification with the perpetrator is established.

5

⁓

Identification with the Aggressor

Finally I just gave up and became my father, his greased, defeated
face shining toward anyone I looked at, his mud-brown eyes in my
face, glistening like wet ground that things you love have fallen
onto and been lost for good.

—Sharon Olds, "Fate"

In 1932, Sandor Ferenczi, an Hungarian-born psychoanalyst,
presented a paper to the Twelfth International Pscychoanalytic
Congress entitled, "The Passion of Adults and Their Influence
on the Sexual Character of Children."[1] This paper, later published as "Confusion of Tongues Between Adults and Children,"
confirmed Freud's original hypothesis that hysteria in adults
could be traced to childhood sexual trauma.[2] Challenging his
colleagues to accept that children "fall victim to real violence or
rape much more often than one dared to suppose," Ferenczi elaborated on those personality characteristics that he attributed to
the trauma of sexual abuse.[3] In particular, he stressed the child's
identification with the aggressor:

It is difficult to imagine the behavior and the emotions of children
after such violence. One would expect the first impulse to be that of
reaction, hatred, disgust, and energetic refusal.... this or something

similar would be the immediate reaction if it had not been paralyzed by enormous anxiety. . . . the real and undeveloped personality reacts to sudden unpleasure not by defense, but by anxiety-ridden identification and by introjection of the menacing aggressor.[4]

Ferenczi's theory of childhood sexual trauma provides a starting point from which to examine the victimized daughter's identification with her abusive father, an identification that has important implications for a gendered understanding of female development. Theories of gender identification and sex role learning tend to focus on the daughter's relationship to her mother, assuming a somewhat continuous attachment from early childhood into adolescence.[5] Sexual violence, however, destroys this pattern of development, shifting the daughter's object of identification from mother to father. Within Ferenczi's theoretical framework, the empathic attachment to the perpetrator discussed in the previous chapter is one manifestation of this shift in identification. Two other aspects that will be elaborated on here are the internalization of the male ego ideal and the introjection of the aggressor, both of which involve the daughter's identification with and desire for the power and personal agency associated with male culture in general and the powerful abusive father in particular.

The Internalization of the Male Ego Ideal and the Rejection of the Female Self

In a contemporary feminist analysis of psychoanalytic theory, Jessica Benjamin suggests that fathers in patriarchal culture are the idealized identificatory parent for both girls and boys. Writing in *The Bonds of Love*, she states:

Briefly, this is what I propose: what Freud called penis envy, the little girl's masculine orientation, really reflects the wish of the toddler—of either sex—to identify with the father, who is perceived as representing the outside world. Psychoanalysis has recognized the importance of the boy's early love for the father in forming his sense of agency and desire; but it has not assigned a parallel importance to the girl's. This early love of the father is an "ideal love": the child idealizes the father because the father is the magical mirror that reflects the self as it wants to be.[6]

According to this perspective, the father is the ego ideal (the representation of perfection) for both male and female children who identify personal agency with the gender of the more powerful parent. Especially for the victimized daughter, the male ego ideal assumes particular importance as her identification with the father is informed by the boundary violations of traumatic sexualization and the absence of a strong identificatory relationship with the mother in the abusive family. As a result, the abused female child may develop what Benjamin terms a "fraudulent" identity[7] that becomes evident in fantasies of maleness and the imitation and modeling of the father to the exclusion of the mother. Each of these attributes of male identification significantly inform the daughter's personality.

Female Personality Development and the Fantasy of Maleness

In the formation of personality, fantasy becomes an important aspect of identification that occurs in the development of the ego ideal.[8] Through fantasy, the victimized female child may reconstruct herself in the image of idealized male perfection. Thus, as E. Sue Blume suggests, the victimized daughter reinvents herself through her identification with the gender of the perpetrator:

> . . . child victims often recreate *themselves*, developing alter egos who offer a positive life alternative to their own. Most commonly, this is a male persona: female survivor clients may either substitute

alternative male personalities, or attach to a male fantasy companion. This is simple to understand: as a victim, and a female, she associates her vulnerable state with defenselessness; males, however, are seen as physically stronger, and not easily targeted for victimization.[9]

Accordingly, the incest survivors interviewed for this study reported a rich fantasy life through which they escaped the entrapment of abuse and the constraints of the feminine gender role. In seeking out male-identified personas, the fantasies of the respondents incorporated cultural ideals of maleness that are reflected in the idealized social roles of men both in the family and in the larger society. In particular, themes of heroism, freedom, and adventure contextualized the imaginary world of the survivors. The most common fantasies were those that emphasized heroic acts and brave deeds, as the following account from a twenty-one-year-old, white survivor illustrates:

> In these fantasies I was always rescuing someone from being hurt. A lot of them had to do with riding away on a white horse. There was always a prince in the picture, a savior figure that was a lot older than me. The prince was always on another horse or was helping me rescue someone, or I would rescue someone and he would be there approving.

In this account, the gender role reversal is evident in the respondent's identification with the savior rather than the victim. Here, as in many of the fantasies reported by the women, horses symbolize the freedom and power that are typically associated with male culture in the tradition of European fairy tales and the colonization of the American West. As such, one white survivor, forty years of age, described an imaginary world in which she became the male heroes that she idolized in childhood:

> I would be like the hero. I would fantasize breaking up fights or saving someone. I also used to fantasize riding across country on a

horse. I remember the Hardy Boys from T.V. who were on the ranch. I used to fantasize doing that kind of thing. I used to fantasize being with them, being the big strong person and some catastrophe would happen and I would save everybody and then I would ride off into the sunset and nobody would ever know.

It is significant that the identification with male heroism creates an imaginary self in which the child is empowered to rescue another. Such myths of male protection reflect her own desire to be saved by the ideal father who, at least in fantasy, protects and saves the helpless daughter. This response to victimization has an interesting parallel in those traditions in which the myth of the woman warrior prevails. In Maxine Hong Kingston's autobiographical work, *The Woman Warrior*, the image of the powerful female savior is internalized by young Chinese girls whose mothers would "talk story," creating a masculinized alter ego with which the daughter might identify:

> When we Chinese girls listened to the adults talk-story, we learned that we failed if we grew up to be but wives or slaves. We could be heroines, swordswomen. Even if she had to rage across all China, a swordswoman got even with anybody who hurt her family. . . . Night after night my mother would talk-story until we fell asleep. I couldn't tell where the stories left off and the dreams began, her voice the voice of the heroines in my sleep.[10]

In the myth of the woman warrior the psychic drama of the female shaman is played out in imaginary scenarios of confrontation wherein the Chinese daughter finds within herself the power to battle men who "sat on naked little girls"[11] and ghosts who attack women in their beds at night. Such allusions to sexual violence suggest that perhaps the myth of male power that characterizes the Chinese swordswoman's shamanic journey serves the same function as the fantasies of maleness that pervade the imaginary world of incest survivors. Like the victimized daughters, the woman warriors of Kingston's spiritual heritage are female avengers who battle good and evil, saving the virtuous from the violence and harm of male domination. Yet, these acts of heroism can only be constructed through the image of the masculine persona, an image that is embraced by those who in reality must submit to the oppressors they have idealized.

Among victimized daughters, the myth of the male persona is often played out in childhood games that cast the young girl in the role of her alter ego. As pirates, kings, and soldiers, the abused children achieve a kind of personal agency in the world that is ordinarily the domain of men and boys. As such, one young woman reported that she always wanted to be Tom Sawyer:

> I loved Mark Twain and would always pretend that I was Tom Sawyer. We had a little stream running outside our house and I would cross the stream and build a fort on the other side. I would paddle down the stream with a straw hat and I would be there all day, pondering. I called it pondering because that's what he called it. I really tried to change into him, but it didn't work.

Another woman in her late twenties recalled that her favorite games were those in which she played a boy:

> I had this best friend that lived two doors down and we played this constant game. It was two boys running away, like two boys being in juvenile hall. "Two Lost Boys" is what we called it and I was always the author of the stories we acted out. We had dares we would do, like jumping off a rock into a swimming pool or climbing on high bars. These were kind of risky, on-the-edge games that involved a lot of athletics and nerve.

The masculinized alter ego, as it is elaborated here, bears a certain similarity to the female masculinity complex first described by Freud[12] and later given a feminist interpretation by Karen Horney.[13] Characterized by a rejection of passivity and a refusal to accept the feminine role, this developmental phenomenon is discussed by Horney in a paper entitled "The Masculinity Complex in Women," in which she offered the following observations:

> We see, first of all, apart from a deliberate emphasis of femininity, that the woman in question would have liked to be a boy as a child; we furthermore hear all kinds of complaints about men's better social position and general status. . . . revealing how man is considered high above woman, implying that female is equated with inferior. All sorts of complaints come up, like: I don't like myself the way I am, physically, characterwise, or intellectually. Only a closer look shows us that all these attitudes originate in extensive masculinity desires and fantasies, and are connected with an intense envy of man.[14]

Further, Horney found in her patients evidence for what Freud interpreted as penis envy in women, fantasies of the wounded or maimed female genitals, unconscious images that were charged with strong emotions of fear, guilt, and shame. Because this fear was primarily focused on the father, Horney concluded that the anxiety she observed in her patients was related to unconscious fears of sexual aggression that were Oedipal in nature. So terrifying were these emotions, suggested Horney, that the daughter gives up her father as a love object and rejects the female role.[15]

In this provocative analysis it appears as if Horney is moving closer to a recognition of sexual violence in the lives of the women she treated. Ultimately, however, she relies on Oedipal theory and traditional Freudian analysis to explain the fearful emotions that surround the father. The case of patient Y is especially revealing. Over the course of treatment with Horney, this woman repeatedly spoke of having been raped by her father, a belief that Horney attributed to fantasies of castration:

> I saw this very clearly in the patient Y, whom I have already mentioned more than once. I told you that this patient produced fantasies of rape—fantasies that she regarded as fact—and that

ultimately these related to her father. . . . Her castration fantasies took the familiar form of imagining that she was not normally made in the genital region, and besides this she had a feeling as though she had suffered some injury to the genitals. On both these points she had evolved many ideas chiefly to the effect that these peculiarities were the results of acts of rape.[16]

Had Horney considered the possibility of true rather than imagined violation, perhaps the fearful fantasy of the maimed female genitals would be understood as the legacy of sexual assault on the child's body rather than a symbolic representation of fantasized castration. This understanding of the masculinity complex in women would seem to be a viable interpretation in light of the similarity between Horney's case studies and the accounts of contemporary victims of sexual abuse. Fantasies of maleness which underlie the development of incest survivors are often accompanied by envy of male culture, as Horney described, and the internalization of traits that are defined as masculine. As one twenty-three-year-old respondent from a white working-class family explains:

> I liked being a girl but I wanted some things about me to be like one of the boys. I didn't like being like girls. I tried not to be like a girl, feminine, emotional, because I thought that was stupid. It was worse than stupid, it's really bad to be that. I really wanted to be like a guy, I really learned how not to cry. I was shy and would cry easily. I learned I didn't want to cry ever. I was strong like a man and things didn't affect me. I didn't get bothered or scared. But of course I got scared all the time and lived in fear.

As this account illustrates, the abused daughter experiences a great deal of confusion over her femininity and its association with vulnerability and fear. In rejecting that which is defined as feminine, the victimized daughter embraces a negative identity, a developmental process that Nancy Chodorow has attributed to male children who, in order to construct a sense of self, must deny that which is associated with the female and the maternal.[17] Like the sons of patriarchy, the abused female child must also reject the mother and female identity, a rejection that leads to modeling and imitation of the aggressor.[18]

Social Adaptations to Male Identification

The male-identified alter ego of the daughter often finds expression in social roles that are associated with the status of the aggressor, that aspect of identification that is found in role modeling the idealized parent. In this developmental process, the daughter modifies her behavior and self representations[19] to correspond with the behavior and personality of the father. The account of a twenty-seven-year-old, middle-class survivor speaks to the approval she sought in becoming like the perpetrator:

> I was really rebellious. I really yelled and talked back to my father. There is an unspoken rule that you don't yell at our parents but I yelled back all the time, from as early as I can remember. I think he had more respect for me because I talked back. Sometimes I think he is kind of proud of me for just the way I am, more like him in some ways. I guess I always wanted to be somewhat like my father. He was always responsible, worked hard. But he was a man and there was no way I could grow up to be a man.

In role modeling fathers, the victimized daughter will often excel in those areas which are valued by the perpetrator and thus valued by the culture as a whole. A good example is that of a white, middle-class respondent who excelled in math and science, the subject areas her father taught in high school:

> My father was a math teacher in my school. He was chairman of the math department and very powerful in the high school. My junior and senior year I was very involved in high school, student

activities, and stuff. I was president of the student council so my father and I ran the school together and we were very close. What I realized recently is that we were close when I was doing what he was doing. . . . The only things he sees me being good at is math and a little bit of science. That's the only positive reinforcement that I ever got.

Other survivors reported assuming professions, which like that of the abuser, represented achievement in the male-dominated world. A case in point is a forty-year-old survivor from a working-class background who became a machinist in a predominantly male environment:

I work in a real macho environment. I am the only woman on the shift from 3:00 to 11:00. I can do the job better than any of the guys. We make tools and I work machinery. The atmosphere at work is one that I've learned to live with.

The male-identified achievement of the victimized daughter is in part motivated by the need for approval from the idealized parent. In seeking this approval, the respondents reported that their self-worth was often tied to recognition and validation from the perpetrator. This need for affirmation is expressed by an adult survivor:

It was very important to me that he love me. It was like passage into the world was to be with him. If I couldn't get him to accept me, then there was nothing for me to go out in the world with.

The father's approval, although desperately sought by the child, was rarely obtained by the respondents, as the daughter's gender signified her inferior status both in the abusive family and in the outside world. As such, the desire to be male in childhood was often expressed as the wish to be an idealized son, a boy who the father might respect and who would not be violated. This adaptation to abuse is especially prevalent among those survivors with male siblings. Here a thirty-five-year-old survivor from a white, middle-class background describes the envy she felt toward her brother who held an esteemed position within the family:

> I wanted to be like my brother. I think it is a reaction because of the power imbalance in my family. Seeing my father have so much power and my mother completely disempowered and not wanting to be like my mother. She was weak. She couldn't make decisions. Everything had to be deferred to him. My brother, as he was growing up, had the same status as my father because he was the boy, always praised, the golden boy. And my sisters and I were, well, we were just girls. Yes, I really wanted to be like my brother. He was my role model because he was successful and he was powerful.

For the abused daughter, the favored son symbolizes the male ego ideal, as his position and status within the family reflects the desire for power and control that is the privilege of her brother's gender. Such sibling envy is not of course confined to incest survivors but is symptomatic of many daughters who are raised within the framework of patriarchal family relations that privilege sons. The envy of the abuse victim, however, and her intense identification with her male sibling, assumes a special quality of idealization as her brother provides a concrete role model against which to assess her own vulnerability and deficiencies and thus to construct an alternative identity. The idealized brother may thus become the hero around which fantasies of the male persona are created. The following account will help to illustrate this phenomenon:

> I am still not sure I don't want to be my brother. He's gorgeous. That's how my mother refers to us—as her perfect child and the one that is opposite. I'm the opposite. My brother's my hero. He's always been very beautiful and social. He was really popular at school and I was kind of a misfit, so he would troubleshoot for me in one area and I would troubleshoot for him in another. If he

would get punished I would jump in and get it instead of him because I couldn't stand for him to be punished.

Such idealization arises out of the wounded child's self percep-tion as she internalizes a scarred image of the female self which is only partially displaced by the alter ego of a fantasized male iden-tity. It is not surprising then that survivors frequently assume a "tomboy" persona which informs the core identity of the female child. This fantasy of maleness, however, is painfully shattered at puberty when the daughter's changing body reminds her that she is both female and powerless.

The Male Ego Ideal and the Devaluation of the Female Body

While puberty represents a painful time for many adolescent girls, for daughters in incest families this transition into female adulthood may be especially difficult and confusing as her body signals not only the passage into female adulthood but the recog-nition that the internalized masculine ideal is truly a fantasy of other and can never be the real self. While some survivors nev-ertheless welcome this change, the majority of the women interviewed expressed an ambivalence over adolescent develop-ment that was frequently characterized by a rejection of the female body. In some cases this rejection was manifested in the development of an athletic physique which, for the abused daughter, mirrored an ideal of maleness. A twenty-two-year-old, white respondent from an upper-middle-class family remembered the pride she took in her muscular image:

I can only feel proud of my body if I have a lot of muscles. Because I was a gymnast, I thought it was great. I'd walk into the weight room at my high school and there would be these guys in there . . . and I remember someone saying, God, you look like a male swimmer. They were looking at my shoulders and I would say, thank you. I think that was a big part of body building. I was not soft. I was not feminine. I'd walk bow-legged and all of that to be tough.

Those daughters who constructed an identity in the image of the ideal boy child expressed hatred and disdain for the women they were becoming in adolescence. Here, a twenty-nine-year-old respondent, assaulted before the age of four, described her angry response to womanhood:

I was always such a tomboy and everything. I remember telling my mother that I didn't want to grow up. She said why and I didn't understand why, but I just didn't want to grow up. I decided it was almost a betrayal sort of thing. I remember my Mom saying, you really must wear a bra and I didn't want to. I just didn't want to. I'd wear it to school and take it off and hide it in my coat pocket and try to remember to put it back on. I remember just suffering. I was not happy about it. I didn't want this transition.

Another respondent described similar feelings of denial and betrayal at the onset of menstruation:

I hated it. I was so ashamed. I cried when I got my period. Sobbed. Sat on the toilet and cried. I was so sensitive about it. I got it when I was twelve. I'd already been abused. I begged my mother not to tell my father. She said she would have to tell him sometime, but not right now. I had horrible cramps with it. It was a very painful experience for me and I just hated pubic hair. I was a dancer and in eighth grade I really got into being a dancer and began to purge a lot and make myself throw up. I had a beautiful body but just detested it. I wanted a dancer's body, which was flat chest, no ass, long neck, very child looking and boy looking. . . . I used to shave my pubic hair right off, I hated it.

Still, for others, menstruation signaled disappointment and resignation:

> I felt really disappointed when I started my period. I felt like some-
> how there was a part of myself that wasn't the same anymore. It
> was clear that I was absolutely a girl. I even flashed on my father
> because now I wouldn't be a tomboy anymore. My father wanted a
> boy and I tried to live up to the tomboy type of image.

The rejection of the female self evident in the suffering and
anger experienced at puberty may help to explain the prevalence
of eating disorders among incest survivors.[20] The research on
anorexia and bulimia[21] suggests that this pattern of behavior is a
form of control that the adolescent girl seeks over her body. As
such, Jane Ussher describes the relationship between the onset
of menstruation and anorexia:

> It is at this stage that a major split can develop between body and
> self (Orbach, 1986) as the young woman develops insecurities
> about a body which is seemingly out of control. . . . In the most
> extreme cases this sense of splitting, the loss of control, can result
> in anorexia nervosa. This may be the only way in which the ado-
> lescent can regain the control which she seems to have lost, to
> achieve the ideal, as she perceives it, of feminine beauty, the thin,
> boyish figure. The first menstrual period plays an important part in
> this illness, as the body can seem to be further out of the control of
> the young woman.[22]

For the incest survivor, her body becomes the symbol of her victimization and thus the focus of her desire for control. Further,
the obsession with a thin, boyish body, rather than an expression
of femininity, may represent an unconscious rejection of the
female self through which the daughter attempts to integrate the
internalized male ego ideal with an external image of a masculinized child's body. Because eating disorders can result in
amenorrhea (the cessation of menstruation), the daughter
achieves what perhaps is an unconscious desire to be male.

The effects of male idealization combined with the devaluation
of the female persona results in a dichotomized representation of

self: that which is valued becomes associated with the aggressor; that which is denigrated is personified by the victim. This dichotomy is further reinforced by the social reality of the incestuous family as well as the larger culture in which the violent family resides. Within the family, the mother, who may herself be victimized, is subservient and fearful of the father. Outside the family, women are objectified, discounted, and are frequently the victims of violence. The choice to identify with the aggressor thus appears to be a rational as well as unconscious act of salvation, a conclusion that Horney also draws in her analysis of the role that social forces play in shaping the male-identified female persona:

> Above all, elements driving her away from her female role on the deepest instinctual level are supplied with elements that *attract* her to the male side on a conscious level. For we live, as George Simmel has put it, in a male culture, i.e. state, economy, art and science are creations of man and thus filled with his spirit.[23]

The Internalization of the Aggressor

For the abused daughter, the male ego ideal embodies a complicated set of associations that reflect the contradictions of a culture wherein male strength and violence both free the helpless and oppress the powerless. Thus, the savior and the perpetrator are one in the same, masculine and powerful. Accordingly, the identification with the abusive father reflects the split in the daughter's male identification, as the ideal of male virtue coexists with the introjected male aggressor. It is therefore not only an ideal of masculinity which informs the development of the female self, but the violence and aggression of the perpetrator as well. Through the attachment and identification with the abuser, the violence of the father is merged with the repressed anger and rage of the victimized daughter, further confusing the boundaries between the self and the more powerful other.

Rage and the Internalized Aggressor

Through an identification with the violent perpetrator, the sexually victimized daughter may engage in fantasies of aggression as well as behaviors that replicate the violence of the father. The existing research on incest suggests that female victims tend to turn aggression inward toward themselves, while males tend to direct their aggression outward toward others.[24] According to Christine Courtois, female incest survivors may engage in a variety of self damaging behaviors, including self-neglect and self-sabotage, addictive and compulsive behaviors, self-mutilation, and suicidal tendencies.[25] Less clearly articulated are those responses to victimization in which the female child assumes the role of the male perpetrator, externalizing her rage through an identification with the aggressor that is more typically associated with victimized males. This identification with power, which acts in defense of the abused daughter's ego, is explained by Anna Freud in her work on child development:

> A child introjects some characteristic of an anxiety-object and so assimilates an anxiety-experience which he [she] has just undergone. Here, the mechanism of identification or introjection is combined with a second important mechanism. By impersonating the aggressor, assuming his attributes or imitating his aggression, the child transforms himself [herself] from the person threatened into the person who makes the threat.[26]

Because the majority of the respondents had experienced multiple traumas, as physical abuse, emotional cruelty, and battering characterized the behavior of the perpetrator in the incest family, the rage and anger of the daughter was manifested in a variety of aggressive responses that ranged from physical assault to forms of sexual abuse that mimicked the violations to which the child had been subjected. According to Leonard Shengold, such identification

enables the former victim to follow the compulsion to repeat, playing the active, sadistic, parental role. This too can be motivated in part by the delusive wish to make the bad parent good: "I'll be father and do it, and *this time* it will be good."[27]

The compulsion to repeat the father's violence, as described by Shengold, is articulated by a working-class survivor whose parenting reflected her identification with the aggressor:

My partner has five kids and when we first started living together, her youngest three were still at home so I walked into the dynamics of this wonderful situation and when I think about how I treated those kids, the boys especially, I feel so much shame and guilt. It was my father all over again, and I was doing exactly what he did to me. Discounting, yelling at us for the slightest thing. It's my father in me that I was acting out. As much as I hated that system, when I look at my personality through those years, I acted it out. I played it. I was the tough guy just like him.

In a somewhat different pattern of repetition, a thirty-five-year-old, white, middle-class respondent recalled her violence against an older sister, a sibling she perceived as weaker and more helpless than herself:

I dominated and was more aggressive toward her, and the way I used to terrorize her, which I feel very sad about now because she still has a real phobia about it, was I would try to strangle her. I had this thing about strangling her and it got to a point where she was so terrified of me strangling her that she couldn't sleep. Now today she can't wear anything around her neck. I have a lot of neck issues too, so I think, in fact, I have thought that my father had his hand around my neck when he was doing things to me, sort of holding me down.

The scapegoating described in this account is not uncommon among victimized children who direct their anger and rage at those who appear less powerful than themselves.[28] In this case, the sister's passivity and helplessness in the face of her sibling's aggression, mirrored the helplessness of the respondent in the face of her father's incestuous assaults. In internalizing the aggressor, a pattern of violence thus emerges which manifests an identification with both the perpetrator and the victim, as the violence against the weaker sibling signifies violence against the victimized self. Another example of this form of projective identification is described by a seventeen-year-old, Latina survivor from a working-class background:

> My first fight was with this girl. Her dad was a biker. He was really heavy and he beat up on her, and we got into this fight and it last-ed an hour and a half. . . . That girl, her stepdad, he molested her. I feel sorry about that, but I have so much anger toward her. Already in my dreams I've killed her, and that's bad, having it in your dreams.

Here, again, an abused child becomes representative of the violated self. Thus, in this survivor's rage, she assumes the role of the aggressor, wishing to annihilate the young girl who like herself had been victimized.

The adolescent respondent quoted above, like a number of teenage survivors in the study, found an outlet for her aggression in the culture of violence that pervaded her peer group interactions. Especially for young women of color who were raised in neighborhoods where gang violence is pervasive, membership in teenage gangs provided the victimized daughter with a social identity that reinforced her identification with the aggressor. A young Latina respondent described this socially constructed identity:

> My boyfriend was a skinhead. I was a skinbird. We'd always get into fights. I got suspended from school for fighting and I had to go

to court once. When I got pregnant things really started to change.
I just got tired of it because all they did was beat each other up.

As this account suggests, the male-identified world of teenage
girls also becomes the arena in which introjected aggression is
played out and reinforced. Accordingly, a recent study of incest
and teenage behavioral problems found a significant relationship
between peer-group reinforcement and aggressive behavior:

> The final areas we examined were those which indicate behavioral
> problems in the girls. The most extreme and significantly different
> behavior between the incest and comparison groups was the social-
> ized aggression dimension, which represents acting out, externalizing
> behavior in the context of a deviant peer group. This result may
> indicate that our sample of incest girls was strongly influenced by
> peers, with a related rejection of authority and society's norms.[29]

While peer interaction provides one social milieu in which to
validate the internalized aggressor, the abusive family represents
another context wherein violence is legitimated and often
rewarded. Attacks against siblings, as described earlier, represent
one manifestation of this intrafamilial power dynamic. Another
manifestation is found in violence which is directed against
mothers in incest families[30] and, in some cases, the perpetrator.
Aggression against the mother was reported by four respondents
in this study and in all cases the assaultive behavior took place
during adolescence. In reporting these incidents, the survivors
expressed guilt and a fear of their own violence. Here a white,
middle-class respondent, now twenty-six, recalled an altercation
with her mother:

> I remember when I was in high school, really breaking away from
> my family. My mother tried to stop me from doing things, and I
> shoved her and I felt what it was like to explode at that point. It
> really frightened me. I thought I was like that, like him and I was
> afraid of that part of me.

Although aggression against mothers tended to erupt in response to conflicts over autonomy, aggression against the perpetrator was more often related to acts of protection involving other family members, including battered mothers and abused siblings. Under these circumstances, the violence of the victimized daughter emerges in response to the victimization of significant others whom the child wishes to protect. A poignant example is that of a seventeen-year-old, white survivor from a poor family who interceded on behalf of her younger sister:

> I have a stepsister but I have been around her most of my life. I protect her. I mean I put my life in harm protecting her. Once when she was getting in a fight with my stepdad I stepped in because I didn't like him hitting her at all. I didn't care if I got hit, it was her I was worried about. I went after him with a knife because I was so scared he was going to do something. I didn't trust him around her. He knows I would kill him. I told him, I said if you ever think of child molesting her, you die.

In this respondent's role as protector, she acts to save her sister from the abuse which she herself had not been spared, matching the violence of the aggressor with her own violent attacks. In attempting to reverse the power between victim and perpetrator, this young survivor becomes the idealized hero of her own inner world as the fantasy of aggressive retribution is actualized in her role as savior.

Such transformations, which may be empowering to the victimized child, may also lead to a split in the daughter's psychological development which in severe and prolonged cases of abuse may lead to multiple personality disorder.[31] This disorder is characterized by a fragmenting of the self into alter personalities. Susan Forward and Craig Buck describe one such case in which the alter personality of an incest survivor revealed her unconscious identification with an incestuous grandfather with whom she lived until his death when she was six years old. As an adult this woman suffered from attacks in which she would lose control and assume an aggressive and abusive personality. Through hypnosis, this survivor discovered the split that had occurred in her development as she struggled to integrate the "little princess" who her grandfather adored with the violent grandfather who assaulted her. Forward and Buck provide this account of the critical hypnotherapy session that revealed the alter personality of the aggressor:

> "Are you his little princess?" asked Hendershaw [the therapist].
> "Yes," she replied in her six-year-old voice.
> "Are you scared?"
> She paused for a moment, as if paralyzed, then suddenly her face distorted into a macabre mask of pain and passion. As Hendershaw stared the voice he had first heard over the phone came out of her twisted mouth.
> "You goddamn son-of-a bitch whore, suck my cock" she screamed in that unearthly rasp. "I'm gonna get you, you shithole, and I'm gonna shove it up your ass."[32]

In this disturbing account of introjection the aggression of the perpetrator-alter is expressed through the imagery and language of sexual violation, an identification with the aggressor that is explicitly linked to acts of sexual violence against the child. Although none of the women interviewed for this study suffered from multiple personality disorder as described above, the reports of the survivors nonetheless indicate that identification with the sexual aggression of the perpetrator was manifested in childhood play and sexual fantasies in which themes of sexual violence and domination were pervasive.

Introjection and Sexualized Aggression

In both childhood play and sexual fantasies survivors describe the presence of a shadow self whose identification with the abuser is manifested in unconscious strivings toward sexual dominance and control that reverse the power dynamic of traumatic sexualization. Therapists who work with abused children often use play and fantasy as a means to ascertain the nature and extent of sexual violence experienced by the child. Similarly, the survivors in this study offered retrospective accounts of play and fantasy that represent the daughter's attempt to integrate and reconstruct the trauma of sexual abuse. A seventeen-year-old, African American respondent from a middle-class background described the way in which the memory of sexual assault was reenacted with a doll that had been given to her soon after she was removed from the abusive family:

> I tore up that doll so bad. She was about as big as me when I was little. She was black like me. I wrote on her face, wrote on her head, put moustaches on her . . . I'd take off her clothes and they would be gone. The doll would be running around naked all the time, all the time. My babies were naked all the time.

This account illustrates the complex nature of the child's identification with the aggressor. In depriving the doll of her clothes, the child becomes the perpetrator, as the unprotected body of the doll signifies the unprotected body of the victimized daughter. At the same time, the young child victim disfigures the face of her beloved "baby," ragefully masculinizing the doll with the physical attribute (the moustache) of the aggressor.

Other accounts of sexualized interactions with toys frequently involved play with Barbie dolls, the plastic embodiment of the ideal female body. Here, a white, twenty-year-old respondent recalled how she would manipulate her Barbie dolls:

> My Barbies would have sex. When we played Barbies all the other girls would ask, what are your Barbies doing? And I would say they are touching each other. I would make them bend and touch their genitals, or at least where their genitals should be.

For some respondents, sexualized play took on increasingly aggressive overtones in interactions with other children.[33] Here the victimized daughter would assume the role of the perpetrator in an unconscious replication of the repressed trauma. One such experience is described by a twenty-eight-year-old survivor from a white, middle-class background who was abused in early childhood:

> I played sex games with other girls. Actually it was a savage type thing, kidnap and tie up and things like that. We took turns tying each other up but I was usually the initiator. And it didn't seem at all unusual or strange at the time. We would pretend to torture each other. As we got older, we started to do really strange things.

Another woman, twenty-three years of age, reported the following:

> My girlfriend and I would play together and I was bigger so I was the man. We were pretty little and I'd pretend like I was the guy and she was the girl and sometimes I would get pretty aggressive and she'd say, don't act like that. But I liked playing that role. I think I even pretended I had a penis. I still have that fantasy. I really feel like it's control. You have some control and you have this thing you can stick out. It's like something you're putting into somebody else. That's what it was always like. I still have this thing about wanting to have a penis because you have more control.

In a further merging with the perpetrator, this same respondent reported a recurrent dream that was very troubling to her:

> I had a really awful dream. It bothered me so much, I wrote it down. I was with a woman but I was being really, really hard on her and really rough and it was just a dream but it was like I was becoming the abuser and I stopped in the middle of it and I said, "God, I'm sorry. I don't even know what I'm doing," and she said, "Well, I like it." But I said,"No, I'm not doing this. This is hurting

you. This is not how I want to do this." Then I was gentle with her, but it was amazing that I was the abuser in that situation and I was hurting her.

The aggressive sexual play that informed this survivor's early life, as well as her fantasies of sexual domination, are replete with images of her identification with the perpetrator. Her desire for a penis cannot be understood apart from the reality of sexual victimization, as the male genital signifies dominance and control over the victimized self. Here penis envy is not only a metaphor for the social power of males, but a symbolic reconstruction of traumatic sexualization in which the penis represents violence, violation, and power over another. Fearing that her own aggressive impulses are like those of the abuser, this survivor is painfully aware of the introjected aggressor who haunts her unconscious.

Other respondents reported fantasies of aggression that involved castration of men, an act of genital violence that may be unconsciously equivocated with the rape of the female body. The following account from a twenty-three-year-old, white survivor illustrates this form of the internalized aggressor:

> I was sitting in class one day and the teacher, he's like a real father image to me but it's also been a kind of sexual attraction. Well, I remember one day sitting in class and I really just wanted to be held by him. All of a sudden it turned real sexual. I was wondering what was going on. I was thinking about it and I started to get really angry because he would always play games with me, tell me to come to his office and then he wouldn't be there. I was really angry and I thought, that fucker, give me a knife. The first thing that came to mind was that I wanted to castrate him.

As this woman describes her feelings for the teacher and his association with the father, her fantasy of nurturance and love shifts to a desire for violence and revenge in which she is transformed from victim to aggressor. Similarly, a younger respondent, seventeen years of age, reported a fantasy life wherein she would alternate between victim and rapist:

> I was just there, talking to my boyfriend, all of a sudden I started picturing these things in my head. It was a trip. I had him tied to the bed with nothing on. I have my clothes on, he didn't. It was weird because all of a sudden I was attacking him, and he couldn't move because I had him handcuffed actually. It was just intense. I was kissing him on his tummy and he just lay there, like what do I do. Then, in this fantasy, he pulled me off of him and he flipped me over and he took all my clothes off with one hand. I couldn't picture no more, but I just might rape him one day.

As this account suggests, the identification with the perpetrator among sexually victimized daughters is never totally complete. In both the play and imagination of the survivors, a tenuous relationship exists between the internalized male abuser and the violated female child, signifying the divided consciousness of sexual victimization. This split in the development of the self becomes most apparent in the tendency toward revictimization that underlies the internalized male aggressor. While the introjection of the perpetrator may at times mask the daughter's identity as victim and thus contribute to the construction of a false persona, patterns of revictimization reveal the extent to which the unprotected and violated female self also informs the personality of the victimized daughter.

6

❧

Revictimization and the Divided Consciousness of Aggression and Abuse

The child victim has no recourse but to bury, hide, and try to forget the experience. But the humiliation will not go away. It festers, poisons and undermines her being. When the offense remains hidden, unanswered and unchallenged, the sexuality, the very biology of the offended child, becomes her shame.

—Florence Rush

The tendency toward revictimization among incest survivors has been well documented in the literature on women and violence.[1] In particular, Diana Russell found that, compared to nonabused women, individuals with histories of sexual abuse were much more likely to experience repeated victimization, including rape, attempted rape, unwanted sexual advances, and physical violence in intimate relationships.[2] The findings of this research suggest similar patterns of revictimization for a majority of respondents. This pattern of repeated abuse reveals the extent to which a divided consciousness may develop within the victimized child, as the identification with the aggressor masks the effects of learned helplessness and boundary confusion that often lead to destructive and dangerous social attachments. One participant described this split in terms of the contradictions between her public world of achievement and her privatized world of intimate violence:

> It was crazy making. Here I was this bright and successful woman. I had this whole public life and yet in my personal relationship I was being abused and terrorized.

The effects of incest on the developing self are thus manifested both in the identification with power and the internalization of powerlessness on the part of the victimized child. The idealization of the perpetrator in combination with the social conditioning of victimization[3] contribute to the development of a female self that, beginning in childhood, is powerless to prevent abuse from the multiple perpetrators who threaten her world. This detrimental consequence of sexual abuse will be examined in relation to the stages of life through which the daughter passes as she moves from child victim to adult survivor.

Sexual Violence in Childhood and Adolescent Social Relations

In the previous chapter on the identification with the abuser, childhood play represented one means through which the victimized daughter sought mastery over her powerlessness. Frequently, the desire for control was expressed in games and fantasies that included other girls and female friends. By comparison, accounts of sexual play with boys manifested very different characteristics as such play tended to become nascent forms of victimization in which the boys assumed control of the interaction, escalating the aggressive quality of the play. It was often in the recollection of these so-called childhood sex games with male children that a survivor would recall her first awareness of the loss of personal agency over her young body. Here, a working-class, African American respondent, seventeen years of age, describes the danger that sexual play represented in her early childhood:

> I remember my babysitter's son. He would always get on top of me from behind—doing sex like playing doggie. I remember that real well cause I was just like a little kid and I just let him do it. And sometimes he would play hide and go-get. It's a game where people catch you and then they get to do it to you if you get caught. He caught me and took me up to his room and he said, "lay down." Then I got scared but it was too late to run away so I had to just let him touch me. But I was scared.

As the abused daughter moves closer to adolescence, increasingly violent sex games are often the arena in which repressed trauma is reexperienced. The account of a twenty-one-year-old, white, middle-class survivor offers insight into the relationship between sexualized play and early forms of revictimization:

> All through grammar school I used to play these sex games with neighborhood boys. I think that's normal but it continued past a point where it was healthy. It degenerated into not just two of us, but it included my best friend, Lisa, and anywhere between four and ten boys. There was kissing and letting them do basically whatever they wanted. We had limits, arbitrary limits, like you can't go inside the pants. They never penetrated us but it definitely got out of hand where I was fighting to get them off, to say this is too much. I enjoyed their attention, the affection I liked, but then it just got out of hand. . . . I was still hanging on to the idea that if I had their attention I was going to get power and respect in some way. And then talking about opposites, of course, I was labeled a slut. I hated that reputation. I hated that things got out of hand, having six, seven boys on you at once is really just too much. When I got to high school, I tried to stop.

This account of childhood victimization poignantly illustrates the way in which sexual objectification is perceived as a means of gaining attention and thus the respect and power of the dominant culture. Such perceptions, which emerge out of the sexualized relationship with the father, result in behaviors that are often labeled as promiscuous,[4] further intensifying the self-blame of the daughter who, like the respondent quoted above, internalizes the shame and self-hatred that accompanies exploitive sexual relations. Another respondent, twenty-three years of age, articulated this self-blame in the following way:

> Of course I could never control myself. It was like I was not supposed to have sex, not do all this stuff, but I couldn't stop myself. I was so promiscuous from the time I was twelve until I was twenty. I couldn't control it. I just couldn't. I needed attention and it was how I dealt with it . . . I went to a Christian school where no one was having sex when they were twelve years old. I felt like a prostitute because I didn't just have sex. Sometimes people would take me into the back room and want to kiss me, or stick their hands in my pants, or fondle me. One time in study hall, I remember I was sitting on the window sill and some guy came up and stuck his hand down my pants and I didn't have a clue. It sounds so dumb because I never did anything to stop them, but I didn't have a clue that you were supposed to. This was the spring before I had sexual intercourse, the spring before seventh grade.

For this respondent, as for many survivors, the need for attention is infused with the patterns of learned helplessness that are associated with the social conditioning of incest perpetration.[5] Deprived of her right to bodily control and integrity, the child is powerless to prevent the boundary violations that accompany sexual exploitation by others, even those violations which are perpetrated by children. In some cases, this effect of incest may lead to a series of degrading and humiliating sexual experiences, as the following account illustrates:

The first time I had sex was with this guy in my neighborhood. He was a delinquent. All the guys in my neighborhood had records and were on probation. He was one of the grossest ones but of course I liked him because he was dangerous. That day I wasn't sure we were going to have sex. That happened to me so many times, where I wouldn't realize what was going to happen. I didn't think we were going to have sex like that. It was really painful. We were at his house and his friend came into the room. I was thirteen, a kid and he was on top of me and he was talking with this guy while he was fucking me. He said, "Come on, do you want a piece?" And the other guy said, "Sure." So Tommy got off and Joey got on and I didn't know I could do anything about it. I didn't have any concept that I could do anything about it so I just let it happen. It was so totally humiliating. I didn't want to have sex but I never said, no. I never thought I could say no.

Among the most pervasive forms of revictimization reported by the respondents in childhood and adolescence are incestuous assaults from male siblings and/or other male relatives. Ten women reported sexual abuse by brothers which included oral penetration, rape, and attempted rape. At the onset of these assaults, the respondents ranged in age from six to nineteen years of age. The frequent occurrence of sibling violence illuminates the extent to which sexual violation becomes a form of normative behavior within the incestuous family. In one such case, a white, thirty-two-year-old respondent described a childhood of physical abuse and sexual molestation by her father who sexualized his sons as well as his daughter:

My dad used to whip us as discipline. We would have to take off our pants and then he would either get a switch or use his belt and whip us. Often times he would make us go one at a time but this time it was Greg and John that were whipped together. . . . They were starting to pull up their pants and my dad said, "no, pull them down again" and John said he just stared at their penises for awhile and then said, "Okay, now you can pull your pants back up now," and then they left.

This survivor reported that molestation by her brothers began when she was about seven years old, at an age in which she had already repressed the memories of her father's earlier incestuous assaults. Throughout her childhood and into early adolescence, she was abused by both of her brothers, beginning with assaults by her older sibling:

> The first thing I can remember was that somebody had come to visit us so that I was not sleeping in my bedroom. I must have been about ten years old. I was sleeping on the couch in the living room and one morning my oldest brother came out and wanted to crawl in bed with me and I thought this was kind of weird but you're raised to be accommodating so it's like, "Oh, okay, well sure." So he did and he started masturbating on me and wanted to feel my breasts. . . . He wanted to kind of feel everything. Before then, he had, when I was seven or eight, done the kind of doctor stuff in the bathroom and had felt my genitals in that area. . . . Now, you've got to understand, Greg was an asshole and he was really volatile like my father, abusive, mean, and I was afraid of him. So there was a power difference that was important here. I would have done what he said and I didn't see the doctor stuff as being so terribly bad but the stuff on the couch was just awful. . . . Then there were subsequent times with Greg, the same kind of thing. Particularly when I would be sleeping at night, he would come in. I had a kind of childhood thing of rocking the bed and I think it would wake him up. This kind of thing went on for about two or three years. I remember then that it would bother me so much that he would come into my room.

That the brother is so strongly identified with the father by this respondent demonstrates the way in which male entitlement pervades the culture of the abusive family and informs the child's submission to her brother's sexual demands. In this case, the

assaults continued for three years until the respondent threatened that God would punish the offending sibling. Although her
older brother stopped molesting her, her younger brother became
more aggressive and his violations were more difficult to reconcile because this brother had been the sibling with whom she felt
closest and most protective:

> When we were growing up, John and I took care of each other. My
> mother was depressed for the first year after I was born and John
> and I were really kind of symbiotic. We liked each other. We were
> both short, fat little blond-headed kids. We understood each other.
> We were emotional support for each other and we were kind to
> each other in a way that no one in the family really was. . . . He's a
> year and a half older than me. When I was getting older he would
> start kissing and chasing me around and actually I've had more
> problems with him than with Greg. I'd lock myself in the bath-
> room until Mom or Dad or someone came home. I was scared of
> John but I knew him better and I liked him, but I didn't under-
> stand what was going on. In some sense it was harder. We were
> supposedly close and I didn't understand why he was doing what
> he was doing because it made me so uncomfortable. I also had a
> much more difficult time being angry at John. I felt sorry for him a
> lot. I tried emotionally to take care of him.

This respondent maintained an empathic connection with her
younger abusive brother until he attempted to rape her one
weekend when she was visiting him at college. Here she
describes the confusion that the assault engendered as she experienced conflicting feelings of outrage and compassion for her
brother:

> He lived in just a one-room place with one bed and no real divi-
> sions of anything and I didn't think too much about that. He said,
> go ahead and take the bed and I did and he slept on the floor and
> that morning he crawled into bed. . . . I mean I was nineteen years
> old. I felt that difficulty of, what do you do? This is my brother. I

care for him. I really like him. He was talking to me very gently and he was telling me about a woman friend who had sexual relations with her brother and that it was okay and he wanted to do that with me and would I mind? I said, "I don't like this. I don't feel real comfortable." He said, "It's okay. It will feel all right." I just kept trying to talk him out of it and I was getting more and more nervous and there was no place for me to go and I didn't know what to do about it. Finally, he started taking my underwear off and crawling on me and started to rape me and I just screamed and shoved him off and just stood there and screamed at him for awhile. I don't even remember how it ended now but classic and typical of my family, however it ended, it blew over. We never talked about it again. We acted as though nothing had happened. We probably did that immediately. It didn't happen.

For this survivor, the incestuous assaults by her siblings were confounded by the empathic attachment that had developed between brother and sister. A similar account of traumatic sexualization by a brother is provided by another woman, thirty-five years of age, whose relationship with her male sibling was characterized by idealization as well as empathy:

When I was putting everything together after these memories from my father, that was something else that fit in. It fit in with the sort of acquaintance rape scenarios of being in a situation and saying no, and not feeling that I could really take a stand on it, or that I could walk away. . . . I think I was about nineteen. I was between nineteen and twenty-one. I had been living in Europe for two years and I came back to the States to visit my family. . . . My brother was living on the east coast then and I'd always had a real close relationship with my brother. In fact, when we were in Asia together and we traveled a lot, people always thought we were husband and wife. We both looked older than we really were and we were so close. We shared the same attitudes and beliefs and we both liked to do the same things. We were both into the counter-culture. He was always my voice, though I was very overshadowed by him. I always thought he was so articulate and brilliant and everything—and he was, but that meant I wasn't developing who I was, so we had always been really close and really shared incredible experiences when we were growing up together.

Anyway, I went to visit him. . . . I was staying with my brother and at that time he was doing massage work so he had a massage table and everything . . . it was summer and it was really hot and I remember being in his apartment and I wanted him to give me a massage or something. I think I had already done it once, or he was doing it for the first time or something, so I was laying naked on his table and he was giving me this massage, doing the points all over my body, and I was laying on my stomach and he was doing the points on the back of my body, and I guess he was getting very turned on by the experience. I don't remember that I was at all, but he was, and so he started rubbing me and massaging me and I remember turning around and looking up and saying, "What are you doing?" And he said, "You know this is kind of interesting. It just seemed like a good thing to do, it just seemed natural, it seemed to sort of fit in with everything." And I said, "Well, I don't know, you know" . . . and he was sort of into it and I once again sort of felt like I can't really say no to him. So I did sort of protest in the beginning and say, "I don't really want to do this," but he went ahead and so he was inside of me . . . Then afterwards, once again, I felt ashamed and disgusted and weird. . . . I don't think we talked about it for a long time.

The effects of sexual abuse by the brother compounds the original trauma of sexualization by the father, particularly when the male sibling, like the paternal perpetrator, is both nurtured and idealized by the victimized child. In addition, as these case studies suggest, sibling violence often leads to a greater sense of confusion surrounding responsibility for the abuse. In this regard, Christine Courtois writes:

I have observed that guilt and feelings of complicity may be more difficult issues for sisters to resolve than for daughters. . . . Many sisters feel as though their inability to stop their brother amounts to their being the initiator or "asking for it." Another pattern shows up in those families where the boys are clearly more valued than the girls and the children are taught that the girls' responsibility is to serve everyone else in the family.[6]

A similar sense of confusion and culpability is experienced when sexual abuse is perpetrated by other male relatives, such as cousins or uncles, or by close friends of the family who are perceived as having the same power and needs as the incestuous father. One white, teenage respondent, molested by her stepfather from age six to twelve, was also victimized by his closest friend. Unable to defend herself against his sexual advances and escalating demands, he raped her at knife point when she was thirteen. A few months later, her assailant took his own life. The young survivor, now sixteen years of age, internalized responsibility both for the sexual assaults and the abuser's suicide:

After he raped me, I put a complaint into the police without anyone knowing except my grandmother, and two months later they were investigating it and a month later he killed himself, and that's when it all started again; I felt like it was my fault that he killed himself. Then I thought, he deserves it and I felt bad because I thought that. I was mixed up. I'm still mixed up. A lot of times, I'll just sit in my room and wish that I had died.

The trauma of revictimization is thus intensified by feelings of self-blame as the victimized daughter repeatedly finds herself in dangerous and violent circumstances. Acquaintance rape, in particular, leads to feelings of responsibility and shame, as revealed in the following account of sexual assault:

In the summer between my junior and senior year in high school, I was on an exchange program to India. My last night there, these two men took me out. They were probably in their mid-forties, doctors with families who were friends of the family where I was living. They got me drunk and tried to rape me, both at the same time. The only reason that they didn't was because my Indian mother got worried when I didn't get home and she came looking for me and found me in this apartment which they kept as a bachelor type of thing. I had tremendous shame about this incident in my life because I didn't do anything. I didn't get up and leave and walk out of their apartment. I didn't take control of the situation and leave. I had shame about that for a long, long time.

Because the incest trauma is often repressed, the survivor who has no conscious knowledge of her abusive past may come to believe that it is some defect or flaw in her personality that is responsible for the violent encounters that seem to plague her life. As one woman explained:

> For the past three years or so I felt like there is something strange about me that makes men react in this way. I have had a lot of different things happen to me, like being locked in a walk-in cooler by my boss at work when I was sixteen. He did let me out but I was scared. I didn't know how much he was joking and how much he was really threatening. And just this past summer, an old man sat down next to me while I was having lunch. He said, "You're a woman with lust written all over your face, you're like a bitch in heat." That same day this guy came running up to me and said, "Would you like to suck my tootsie roll?" And I was like, what is this? Is it that I really do have lust written all over my face?

The self-perception that the daughter does in fact invite inappropriate and violent behavior, in part, emerges out of feelings of acquiescence that are experienced when the survivor is unable to resist or prevent the assaults which seem to occur repeatedly. In a provocative and insightful discussion of revictimization, Bessel A. van der Kolk explains the learned helplessness of incest survivors as the problem of state dependent learning, a form of conditioning that results in the automatic return to states of powerlessness under conditions of retraumatization. He explains this phenomenon as follows:

Reactivation of past learning is relatively automatic: Contextual stimuli directly evoke stored memories without conscious awareness of the transition. The more similar the contextual stimuli are to conditions prevailing at the time of the original storage of memories, the more likely the probability of retrieval. Both internal states, such as particular affects, or external events reminiscent of earlier trauma thus can trigger a return to feeling as if victims are back in their original traumatizing situation.[7]

This interpretation of state dependent learning suggests that the sexually traumatized daughter, when confronted with a similar abusive context, once again becomes the terrified and overpowered victim of her father's transgression. In this regressive state, each new perpetrator becomes the offending parent while she responds as the powerless and objectified daughter. Because this response may only occur under conditions of revictimization, Van der Kolk maintains that women who suffer early childhood trauma may act competently in all other aspects of their lives, except those which are reminiscent of sexual victimization. His work therefore helps to explain the paradox of the successful and high-achieving survivor who repeatedly finds herself in violent or abusive circumstances.

In addition to his theory of state dependent learning, van der Kolk also raises another important consideration for the prevalence of revictimization among abused daughters. Drawing on Freud's theory of repetition compulsion, he suggests that the violated daughter who has never fully integrated the trauma may unconsciously be drawn to those situations that replicate the original violence.[8] Although such interpretations often lend themselves to victim-blaming, and thus must be approached with caution, this understanding of revictimization provides a link between repressed trauma and the tendency among some survivors to enter into relationships that replicate the power dynamics of incest perpetration and are therefore potentially dangerous and exploitive.[9] The findings of this study suggest that the theory of repetition compulsion may indeed apply to a portion of cases reported by the respondents, particularly those in which the survivor became involved in an intimate relationship where loss of control and powerlessness formed the basis for erotic attachment. This form of revictimization is often ambiguous because of the consensual nature of eroticized violence, a phenomenon that is typically characterized as sadomasochism in the studies of sexuality and voluntary submission.

Consensual Victimization and the Search for the Violated Self

The concept of consensual victimization in intimate relationships is most often studied in relation to the phenomenon of sadomasochism wherein consenting partners engage in acts of dominance and submission through which violence becomes eroticized. Over the last decade, the scholarship on sadomasochism has revealed that such relationships inform homosexual as well as heterosexual relationships in contemporary society.[10] Among the respondents in this study, seven women reported having engaged in a relationship of this type, five of which were with men and two of which were with women. Although the survivors reported that they would sometimes alternate between the role of aggressor and victim in these sexual encounters, the tendency among the respondents studied here was to submit to the control of a more sadistic partner. As such, these case studies of sexual domination shed light on the interrelationship between childhood sexual abuse and the social construction of female masochism.

The term masochism, as it applies to that quality of the female persona which associates pain and suffering with pleasure and self affirmation, has a broad range of interpretations in the history and development of psychoanalytic thought. As Paula Caplan insightfully points out in her book on *The Myth of Women's Masochism,* those female behaviors that have been defined as masochistic include the desire for pain in intimacy as well as acts of nurturing and selflessness that emerge out of sex role socialization. In this regard, Caplan writes:

> What, then, is the behavior that in women has led to their being called masochistic? Much of it is in fact *learned* behavior, the very essence of femininity in Western culture. Girls and women are supposed to be nurturant, selfless (even self-denying), and endlessly patient. . . . What is ignored is that women have been intensively rewarded for behaving in this way and that a strong association has been formed between such behavior and the *pleasure* of the reward (usually someone's approval or an increased sense of their own identity as "feminine" or "womanly").[11]

Essentially, Caplan's argument is that as masochism is conceptualized as selfless and altruistic behavior, all women raised with the social values of patriarchy will manifest this aspect of personality formation which has been defined as feminine. Sexual relationships of dominance and submission can then be understood as the extension of traditional sex-role socialization into the realm of sexuality and eroticism. Thus, Linda Phelps concludes:

> If we come to view male dominated heterosexuality as the only healthy form of sex, it is because we are bombarded with that model for our sexual fantasies long before we experience sex itself. Sexual images of conquest and submission pervade our imagination from an early age and determine how we will later look upon and experience sex.[12]

This important understanding of the relationship between sex-role socialization and the social construction of sexuality points out that such social conditioning occurs through the assimilation of cultural values prior to the female child's knowledge or experience of sexuality. Incest adds yet another dimension to this process of social conditioning through the actual manipulation and violation of the daughter's sexual responsiveness, merging sexual stimulation with powerlessness and violence. One outcome of such abuse is the linking of aggression and sexual pleasure, a response in which the daughter may fantasize the role of the abuser, as discussed in the previous chapter, or she may assume the role of the victim in what may be characterized as mutually agreed-upon sexual relationships in which she consents to be dominated and controlled. An example is that of a twenty-eight-year-old, white survivor who described the following experience:

> I had a relationship for three years and there was some sexual abuse but I didn't even realize that I was being victimized until much later. There were some real S and M type things and at first I kept thinking, this is consensual, maybe I should just try this. I feel safe enough with this person. I was head over heels in love with him and willing to do anything, but he definitely had this weird side. He was into handcuffs and things like that, and bondage, and I'm not even sure what this other thing was called but it was some kind of harness. . . . We spent about a month traveling through Mexico together and we were at this hotel room doing all of this stuff and I was really in pain and wanted him to stop and he didn't. In some ways I felt like that was part of our little sex games but he went beyond the boundaries.

The accounts of sexual submissiveness reported here are consistent with contemporary studies of sadomasochism which conclude that the appearance of pain in intimacy seems to be more important than the actual desire for real harm or suffering.[13] Thus, the consensual victimization that characterizes this form of intimate attachment appears to be an unconscious means through which repressed sexual abuse is reenacted within the boundaries of what is perceived by the survivor to be a safe relationship with an idealized partner. A case in point is that of a thirty-six-year-old, white, middle-class survivor who, for a number of years, maintained an affair with a man whom she idealized as nurturing:

> Les was physically much bigger than me and he had very seductive hands. In fact, his hands were for me the most erotic part of his body. He was really very gentle but there was this dynamic between us that started to take over. It would be as if we were playing a sex game like we were little kids only we weren't kids. He would get into the role and at first it was a real turn-on but then there were times when I got really scared. It would get out of control. He would get more and more physically controlling and I would get more and more submissive. Our entire sexual relationship began to be like that. There was little mutuality after awhile. He would order me to do certain acts and if I hesitated or didn't comply he might threaten to hit me, and once or twice he did actually hit me. Then I would submit and it became real twisted. Now that I am aware of my abuse history, the thing that makes me feel the worst is that there were certain acts of degradation, too humiliating to even speak of, that I would do and would want him to do with me and they were exactly what my stepfather had done to me when I was about four or five. Once I realized that, I just felt sick. I had been using this relationship to tap into my unconscious and it worked because, although both of us were afraid of what we were doing, I also trusted him completely and felt safe with him.

It is evident from this account of revictimization that an idealized relationship with a sadistic partner is often the intimate context through which repressed trauma is reenacted within the bounds of what appears to be a safe relationship. In this case in particular, the compulsion to repeat the trauma was manifested in specific episodes of violence and humiliation that were linked to the actual violations of childhood. A significant aspect of the repetition phenomenon is the perception of safety that underlies the tendency toward sadomasochism, what Jessica Benjamin describes as the opportunity to share psychic pain "in the presence of a trusted other who comprehends the suffering he inflicts."[14] Such trust leads to the discovery of the authentic self, the victimized child buried deep within the psyche of the survivor. Thus, the idealization of the perpetrator is pervasive in relationships of consensual victimization that replicate the original trauma of sexualization. The following account from a twenty-seven-year-old survivor further illustrates the desire for trust and safety that masks the real danger of submissive subjugation:

I moved in with this guy who was a nice guy, real warm and cuddly like a teddy bear, but we had this real weird kind of sex life. He just wanted me to be with him all of the time. He was a carpenter and I ran the business for him and it was a real dependent kind of thing. The problem was that he wanted to make love three or four times a day. He really didn't respect my boundaries. It got to a stage after a while where I didn't like sex at all and I was having it three or four times a day and I had to figure out what was wrong with me. I mean I loved this man but I didn't want to sleep with him. I just couldn't figure out what was wrong so I gave more and more, lost more of myself, and became more of him. Even though there were two of us, there was one self and my self was completely gone. I was just bending to his will and it got weirder and weirder. He got into bondage and using chains and things hanging from the walls and while all of this was going on, I was taking karate and he would come and watch me. Then we would go home and get into this weird sex and it was always a risk. He never actually hurt me. I think he was afraid of me but the risk was in how far he would go, how close he would get to crossing over the line where he would inflict real pain on me.

One final example further emphasizes the illusion of safety and nurturance in sexually victimizing relationships:

This woman I was involved with for about a year was really loving and nurturing in a kind of maternal way. But after a few months, our sexual life took on increasingly dangerous and frightening overtones. Sometimes she would want me to hit her. At first I thought it was because she wanted to be dominated but then I would slap her and she would use this as a pretense for retaliating and her retaliation was always greater than what I had done. The sexual excitement was definitely there for both of us. It scared both of us but it was there. The way she held me down sometimes, it was like she was trying to rape me. It was physical domination. I know that now. I even knew it then. I think it was what drew me to her, but it also terrified me about our relationship.

As these cases illustrate, revictimization emerges out of a desire for connection that becomes contextualized by eroticized submission and violence. Sexual responsiveness is thus contingent upon the loss of self that characterized the invasive attachment between the incestuous father and the abused daughter. Because sexual arousal becomes associated with feelings of guilt and self-hatred, punishing and dominating intimacy characterizes the abusive dynamics of consensual victimization. As the loss of self-control defines the conditions under which the original trauma continues to be replicated in adult life, this loss informs all other aspects of the daughter's sexual development. The victimized self therefore becomes the foundation for the formation of the sexual persona that underlies the personality development of the survivor.

7

The Body as Self

Poor daddy. It's all right. The tools hang on the boards of the tar-papered garage, Marilyn Monroe curls down pink and naked from the calendar. . . . "remember, this is just between you and me. Don't tell anyone. Especially mama."

—Jean Monroe, "California Daughter"

Victimized daughters, like all women in Western industrial soci-eties, develop their sense of self in a culture dominated by images of the sexually objectified female.[1] For the sexually abused child, the cultural portrayals of female objectification and degradation merge with internal representations of the self that have been shaped by the experience of traumatic sexualization. As the shame of her private humiliation is mirrored in the social con-struction of woman as body, the abused child's sense of self becomes tied to her identity as sexual object. The behavioral manifestations of this sexualized persona are evident in descrip-tions of victimized daughters as sexually precocious children and sexually compulsive adolescents. The literature on incest thus often characterizes abused daughters as children who constantly engage in sexual activities, drawing few boundaries in their rela-tionships with others.[2] Although these assessments of sexually abused children may in some cases assume a victim-blaming tone, they nonetheless point out the extent to which the social relations of the victimized daughter are informed by the internalization of the sexually objectified female persona. A twenty-three-year-old, white respondent, violated by her father in early childhood, painfully recalled the memory of her twelve-year-old self, a young girl who could not control her sexuality:

> It started when I was about twelve. I just started having these sexual relations with boys all the time. It was like I couldn't help it. I must have wanted the attention but it was like so sexualized. It must have been the summer before seventh grade. I remember there was this kid and we were in a vacant parking lot and we were on a bicycle and I was on the front. He told me to sit there. He was fingering me and he would tell his friend to do it. These guys were always coming to my window. It was very hard. I was a tease. I'd always flirt with every guy. That's how I felt good.

Because the emergence of sexuality in the adolescent daughter is informed by the earlier experience of traumatic sexualization, arousal and sexual stimulation form an unconscious link to the father/perpetrator, reinforcing the young girl's value as body. Thus, as she begins to assess her self-worth in terms of her sexuality, the daughter may confuse perceptions of personal power with the reality of sexual objectification. In the following account, a twenty-four-year-old survivor explains how sexual exploitation in childhood led to perceptions of personal agency that were tied to her victimized identity:

> I learned early that if I flaunted myself sexually then I could get the admiration of boys and that was where the power was. I was going to be free and sexual and out-do all the other girls in this area. . . . No one told me how it could be used against me, how sex is okay but exploiting it isn't okay, how it can hurt.

In mistaking sexual exploitation for power, this young woman personifies the women that Judith Herman treated, survivors who, like this respondent, equated sexuality with power over others:

> Several other women also spoke of feeling that they have extraordinary powers over others, especially sexual powers over men, and destructive powers over both men and women. . . . These fantasies uniformly date back to the incestuous situation in childhood. In part they represent a defense against the feeling which these women had so often experienced, of being dominated and overwhelmed by their fathers. In part they were expressions of the sense of specialness and privilege they had derived from being their father's favorites.[3]

Closely tied to the feeling of power is the equally pervasive feeling of shame, as exemplified by one white survivor's recollection of her first heterosexual experience:

> It is interesting that the man I lost my virginity to looked like a young replica of my father. I was sixteen. He must have been twenty-three or twenty-four. This was in my drug days and I ran around with a very radical crowd. . . . This guy's name was Dan and he was saying, "I want to sleep with a virgin, I want to make love with a virgin," and he was saying that all night long. And I wasn't that attracted to him, but he was putting the moves on me, and I was feeling so eroticized from the drugs, and I was so curious and everything I just figured well, go ahead, and then when we were actually getting into it, I didn't want to continue, and it was painful and he was very nice about it. He wasn't harsh or forceful or anything. He was very gentle and very loving about it, but I felt disgusted and dirty and shameful. . . . I felt ashamed of myself and that was the way I always felt with sex all these years.

The association of shame with sexuality is also expressed by an eighteen-year-old African American respondent:

> I felt so bad after the first time I had sex with Riley. He wanted to do it more than I did even though I care a lot about him. I was so

ashamed. I felt so dirty, like I smelled all the time. I still don't
enjoy it. It's more like a dutiful thing.

Another survivor, twenty-two years old, painfully recounted
her memories of an incestuous brother and the pressure she
experienced to be sexual with his friends when she was eleven
and twelve years of age:

> My brother said that it was his friend that got him to do it [oral sex]
> with me but his friend used to do it to me, too. So I just felt dirty and
> so gross. His friend pushed me more to do it. I remember he'd say
> mean things and he'd say, "Come on, come on, please. I'll give you
> this, I'll give you that," and so I'd finally do it and then I'd just feel
> so gross. Like I was a prostitute then. That's all I thought. . . . They
> used to go around singing "incest is best." They were so crude.
> They were so mean. I remember one time after my brother's friend
> did it to me, he was out on the street and my brother and other
> guys were around and he said, "Oh, I got cunt juice all over my
> mouth." I was there and I was so humiliated I just wanted to cry
> and just die. I was so humiliated by that.

Because of the child's confusion over sexuality and boundary
violations, intense feelings of shame underlie the victimized
daughter's sense of her developing self. As such, E. Sue Blume
maintains that shame is the feeling state through which the survivor comes to define herself:

> Shame is a deeper sense of worthlessness, a sense of inner, innate
> badness, not in relation to one's actions but one's very self. The
> child victim of incest feels shame as well as guilt. We feel guilt for
> what we have done, but shamed by what we are.[4]

Accordingly, a white, middle-class respondent described the disdain in which she held herself as she went from one sexual
relationship to another, searching for validation and a realization
of her sexual power:

I just thought I was nothing. I thought I was gross. I knew it was not normal to do that stuff but I did it through my freshman year in college. I slept around a lot and my friends didn't always like me for it. I never thought anybody would actually like me for who I was and I felt ashamed because of that.

Traumatic sexualization thus conditions the daughter to value herself as body, an internalized objectification that confounds shame with a distorted sense of sexual power. The shame that comes to define the daughter's sense of self, although reinforced by the heterosexual social relations of adolescence, originates with the traumatized daughter's identification with the perpetrator. Sandor Ferenczi explains this aspect of introjection:

> The most important change, produced in the mind of the child by the anxiety-fear-ridden identification with the adult partner, is the *introjection of the guilt feelings of the adult* which makes hitherto harmless play appear as a punishable offense.
>
> When the child recovers from such an attack he [she] feels enormously confused, in fact, split—innocent and culpable at the same time—and his [her] confidence in the testimony of his [her] own sense is broken. Moreover, the harsh behavior of the adult partner tormented and made angry by his remorse renders the child still more conscious of his [her] own guilt and still more ashamed.[5]

For the emergent female self, the loss of autonomy is staggering. Deprived of her body, her empathy, and her identity as separate other, the daughter must now also bear the burden of guilt for the father who has taken everything from her. As the sins of the father truly become the sins of the daughter, shame is the context through which the child comes to know the self as body. Further, the shame of the perpetrator is reinforced by the shame of the child who experiences a loss of control in the presence of the dominating parent. Especially in those cases where sexual violence leads to unwanted feelings of pleasure, the shame of incest is particularly acute. Such responses to overstimulation are perhaps the most difficult for the daughter to reconcile, as evidenced by the account of one young survivor:

> I wanted affection from him and the hardest thing I have had to deal with was that on two occasions I felt pleasure. My body responded. I know it happens all the time, but it is still the hardest thing to get over. He never hugged me, ever, and even when the abuse was over, even more so, I could count on my hands in a year how many times he hugged me. The only time he touched me was in an abusive situation and I remember him saying he wanted to bring me to orgasm. . . . He was violent and he hit me, but never while he was abusing me. Those were separate. He would say things like, "Don't be ashamed of this because there is a famous psychiatrist, Freud, who says that all little girls love their daddies and all daddies love their little girls and it's okay to do this." So he would tell me things like, "I want to bring you to orgasm. I want you to experience this," which was really confusing to me.

This account convincingly illustrates what Alice Miller has termed "poisonous pedagogy," the phenomenon of abuse whereby adult culture legitimates violence against children through the distortion and manipulation of theories of human behavior.[6] Accordingly, Miller writes:

> The child seeks the adults' love because he [she] cannot live without it; he [she] meets all their demands to the extent that he [she] is able—for the sake of survival. He [she] loves his [her] parents, needs their presence, concern, and affection, and will learn to fit his [her] attempt to win these indispensable treasures into the framework provided him [her] by his [her] parents from birth. A child who has been stimulated sexually from the beginning . . . may under certain circumstances come to regard this type of activity as love because he [she] knows no other form of it. But to brand

the child's *reactive* desires as blameworthy, as implied in the drive theory, is undeniably a remnant of the ideology of "poisonous pedagogy," which enables adults to delegate their guilt feelings to the child with the aid of various theories.[7]

Particularly in those cases where feelings of pleasure are associated with a prolonged victimizing experience, survivors may feel especially complicitous, as one women reported: "Although I thought all these years my disgust is for my father, I now realize my disgust is for my own participation and the pleasure I got out of something I accepted as wrong."[8] While the survivor is not responsible or blameworthy, the erotic sensations that sometimes pervade the memories of sexual abuse often generate a great deal of shame for the daughter who, in bringing incest to consciousness, reexperiences the feelings of arousal that are associated with the trauma of sexualization. As one adult survivor explained:

> There was this horrible rape by my stepfather and even after I remembered the actual assault and right before, when I began to have flashbacks, I had these feelings of being turned on, sexually aroused. And I could see his hand on my genitals and I could feel him rubbing me and I could hear his voice. I couldn't believe I was having these erotic feelings and then I would fantasize his touching me and I would see his face and I would have an orgasm. It was almost like I felt possessed, like I had to masturbate and complete the cycle or he would be there in my unconcious forever. Masturbation felt like an exorcism.

In part the shame of incest is the shame of experiencing pleasure at the will and domination of another. Just as the daughter's body has been taken from her, her sexuality is conditioned by the control of the more powerful other; hence, the experience of submission may become merged with feelings of love and the erotic in the unconscious of the victimized daughter.

Stolen Desire and the Violated Self

Incest represents the most extreme conditions under which the sexuality of a female child is socially constructed by the power of male violence and control. This outcome of sexual trauma is evident in the daughter's association of violence and domination with sexual arousal and stimulation. In a revealing recollection of childhood memories, a thirty-two-year-old respondent from a white, middle-class background offered this perspective on the relationship between incest perpetration and the social construction of female sexuality:

> This is how the abuse earlier in my life comes into play. When I was really young my family had gone to a circus of some kind. It was like an arena type thing and there was a pool down there and a man was trying to tame an alligator. First the alligator was really angry and doing all different kinds of moves and the way the man tamed it was to get it on its back and start rubbing its belly. I remember I sat there just petrified. Recently, I realized that all of my major fantasies are variations on that image, of me being upset, being calmed down, having someone rub my stomach, and then being stimulated genitally until I orgasm. Since I started remembering, I also see my father's face, the look on his face when I orgasm, of the sadistic pleasure, like, "see what I can make her do?"

For this victimized daughter, desire cannot be separated from the sadism of the abuser and thus she experiences the pleasure of her body through the fantasy of violation. The themes that pervade such fantasies suggest a pattern of submission and loss of control which is frequently but not always accompanied by violent images of rape, as illustrated by the following account:

> Some of my fantasies have been sort of abusive towards me. I've had fantasies of being dominated, being raped, not being bloody or extremely violent, but definitely having my power taken away. . . .

Here I am a feminist and yet it's very easy for me to have an orgasm if I think of an abusive fantasy, but if I try to think of something loving I don't get anywhere.

The sexual fantasies of the survivors, when framed within the contemporary discourse on female sexuality, suggest that the desire for domination is not limited to sexually victimized daughters but defines the sexuality of all women whose desire has been constructed within the social framework of male dominant culture. Writing on women and "the problem of domination," Benjamin concludes:

Too often, woman's desire is expressed through such alienated forms of submission and envy, the products of idealization. . . . in which recognition is not subject-to-subject but occurs through identification with the ideal; and the erotic relationship is organized into the complementarity of active and passive organs, subject and object of desire. Yet even then, the underlying wish for recognition of one's own desire remains.[9]

What therefore distinguishes the victim of sexual abuse is not her pleasure in submission but the images of brutality that inform her fantasies of objectification.[10] In the most violent of these scenarios, the boundaries between pain and pleasure may become blurred, as the following report from a twenty-six-year-old survivor illustrates:

I have sexual fantasies that involve injuries mostly to women. I read a lot of paperback fiction, trash you can find at the low end of the scale. I would have visual images that these books inspired. I might picture myself getting stabbed or shot. During these fantasies, I can really feel pain, or sometimes I just watch other women being hurt.

Although the sexual fantasies of the survivors tended to eroticize violence and humiliation, with the exception of the few cases of sadomasochism described in the previous chapter, these images were rarely actualized by the women in the study. Rather, it would seem that fantasies, because they are contained by the imagination of the survivor, become a safe psychic arena in which to reexperience and feel the sexual stimuli that are associated with fear and submission. Further, for a small number of respondents, sexual fantasies also manifest the daughter's identification with the gender of the perpetrator as the fantasized object of desire is cast in the image of a tormented male child. One survivor thus spoke of recurring erotic fantasies in which a young boy is victimized by a group of men:

> Many of the fantasies that I use in coming are not of me being a little girl but of me being a boy and being stimulated. And they're mostly humiliating situations where someone is in control over me and I, as this little boy with a penis, can't help myself. . . . It is very coercive but under the guise of being kind of nice, or, let me show you this. For example, did you ever read James Michener's *The Drifters?* Now, I may have it wrong because it's now gone through my fantasizing and I haven't read it for years. . . . There's a boy who somehow ends up with a group of homosexual men and is stimulated with a feather or something and to his surprise, he becomes very sexually aroused and the men are getting off on the fact that he's very sexually aroused and comes to orgasm. That's a real common fantasy of mine, that I'm in a situation where somebody is stimulating me, I'm surprised that it's happening. I'm aware that people around me are being very sexually aroused. I feel like there's nothing I can do about it, that I'm out of control in that sense and then I have an orgasm.

This case is especially illustrative of the daughter's creative adaptation to abuse, as the erotic imagination of the survivor transforms the trauma of fear and over stimulation into a fantasy where unexpected pleasure is derived. Such pleasure results from the stimulation not of her female body but of the imagined male penis. Thus, the identification with the perpetrator reaches far into the unconscious of the victimized daughter whose sexual vulnerability is cast in the image of the idealized male.

Sexual fantasies such as those described above may form a significant aspect of the survivor's sexuality, allowing the traumatized individual to safely experience the loss of control that can lead to arousal. In this world of erotic fantasy, victimization is not relinquished but reenacted as the daughter discovers her sexual self through a reengagement with humiliation and subjugation which, in fantasy, remains within her control. This response to traumatic sexualization represents one form of self-alienation that develops out of incestuous assault. A second form of alienation, equally as damaging, is the survivor's denial of the sexual self, an adaptation to abuse that results in the daughter's disconnection from her body and the physical sensations that remind her of the coerced pleasure and feared pain of incest perpetration.

The Denial of the Self as Body

Through the trauma of incest, the victimized daughter learns that her body represents danger and vulnerability. Unable to protect herself from the sexual and physical assaults of her father, her only recourse from victimization may be found in her ability to dissociate from the traumatic situation. With dissociation, normal awareness is transformed through an alteration in consciousness whereby the child "leaves her body" during the act of sexual violence.[11] This psychological adaptation to trauma allows victimized children to "blank out and be somewhere else in their minds."[12] Research on dissociative responses suggests that this is a complex psychological coping mechanism that serves to protect the child from an unbearable reality. In this regard, Christine Courtois writes:

Dissociating serves many purposes. It provides a way out of the intolerable and psychologically incongruous situation (double-bind), it erects memory barriers (amnesia) to keep painful events and memories out of awareness, it functions as an analgesic to prevent feeling pain, it allows escape from experiencing the event and from responsibility/guilt, and it may serve as a hypnotic negation of the sense of self. The child may begin by using the dissociative mechanism spontaneously and sporadically. With repeated victimization and double-bind injunctions, it becomes chronic. It may further become an autonomous process as the individual ages. Dissociation is therefore another type of survival mechanism used by the child.[13]

In this state of separate realities, the child may watch what is happening to her as if she were outside her body. A twenty-eight-year-old, white, middle-class survivor described this memory of the mind/body split that she experienced during an assault in early childhood:

> I was having a flashback but I didn't want to see it. I would see pictures of me leaning over the bathtub, you know, the edge of the tub, and I saw a flashback from above. My father entering me from behind, having anal sex. It was like I was looking down from above. And I was looking at this picture and I didn't actually see me. I saw a little girl who looks like me, with blond curly hair like mine, but it's like looking at someone else. But I know it's me.

This tendency toward dissociation may continue throughout the individual's life,[14] assuming the quality of an autohypnotic response that Leonard Shengold describes as follows:

> A young woman, who as a child of five had been seduced by an adult male, was subject to repetitive, contradictory states that involved alterations of consciousness. During these periods of perceptible autohypnosis, there was a simultaneous shutting off of emotion and perception. . . . She could at the same moment both block out and be hyperaware of inner reality, outer reality or both.[15]

When threatened or retraumatized, the victimized daughter may reenter this altered state of consciousness. One example is that of a survivor from a working-class background who was violated by her father in early childhood and later assaulted by a step-brother:

> When my mother remarried, this stepbrother was close in age to me. I'm not sure why I was singled out. There were lots of kids in the family. I was probably about nine or ten. He was always making advances towards me in a real adolescent way and I felt afraid. I felt I was always being looked at in a way that made me feel really uncomfortable. My other stepbrothers and stepsisters were there when the incident happened that I clearly remember. It was sort of a provocation, like we dare you to do this. They were all around. I remember he kind of raped me, there was penetration and everyone was there watching. I remember just feeling real disconnected from myself at that point, like I had gone somewhere else.

The tendency toward dissociation may also be present in non-threatening circumstances. Because sexual interaction is itself tainted by the unconscious presence of the incestuous father, the dissociative response may become a pervasive aspect of the daughter's developing sexuality. In *The Courage to Heal*, Laura Davis offers a personal account of her struggle with sexual intimacy in a relationship in which she felt both loved and valued. Here she describes the feelings of passion and loss that she experienced while making love with her partner:

> She was kissing me now, teasing and slow, waiting for me to answer, for me to rise, for me to catch the rush, like winds in a sail, to fly with her. "So far, so good." I thought, my tongue answering, responding, my body firm against hers, passion rising. . . .
>
> And then I felt it. Subtle, unmistakable. Painfully familiar. A small spark of terror and then the screen. An impermeable wall suddenly cast between us, my body cut loose, my mind floating free. I tried to call myself back, but already it was too late. I was

gone. . . . I closed my eyes, tried again to reel myself in. "C'mon Laura. You want to be here. You want to do this. Get back in your body. C'mon! This is the woman you love!"

But it didn't work. My mind was already far above my body, spinning, dancing intricate loops. I felt totally out of control. My body lay on the bed beneath, still going through the motions. God, how I hated this. The old grief, this lack of presence, surged through me.[16]

In this moving recollection, Davis speaks of an impermeable screen that suddenly descends as she detaches from the feelings of desire and passion that are too threatening to sustain. Similarly, other women describe a numbing or shutting down in response to sexual feelings, as the following account illustrates:

I would be in a sexual situation and then I couldn't feel anything in my body. There was just no feeling. I think I could do it consciously, just shut down.

As sexual intimacy creates an unconscious association with the repressed trauma of childhood victimization, the experience of shutting down may become a defining characteristic of the daughter's sexuality.[17] The following account from a twenty-one-year-old respondent expresses the extent to which incest may alienate the survivor from her body:

I lost my virginity when I was fifteen and was very intoxicated. I remember sitting on the toilet afterwards and thinking, that's not a big deal at all, no biggie, totally overrated, because I felt no pleasure. I was drunk and I wasn't even present. Since then all of my other sexual encounters have never been that different. I could have cited the Gettysberg Address while having sex, the alphabet, anything.

In effect, the dissociative response is a flight from body and from the female self that the body signifies. This intrapsychic phenomenon also affords an escape from sexual feelings, the sensations that hold the somatic memories of pain mixed with pleasure and shame. Because sexual arousal represents a dangerous realm within the body that when experienced is a reminder of the loss of control to a more powerful other, the victimized daughter seems to have but two alternatives: to deny her body and thus her victim-self, or to stay present in the realm of the senses and risk experiencing a pleasure that can never totally be her own.

8

ℂ

Change and Transformation: Reconstructing the Female Self

As I dance, whirling and joyous, happier than I've ever been in my life, another bright-faced dancer joins me. We dance and kiss each other and hold each other through the night. The other dancer has obviously come through all right, as I have done. She is beautiful, whole and free. And she is also me.

—Alice Walker

The accounts of survivors, as they have been elaborated throughout this analysis of personality formation, suggest that the concept of survival is perhaps a limited way to understand the developmental struggles that victimized daughters undergo. More than mere survival, the experience of these women also speak to creative adaptation and a willful resistance to the total obliteration of the threatened and traumatized self. Coping with the reality of an abusive childhood, the respondents in this study represent individuals at various stages of recovery, as each of the women struggle to integrate the violence of incest with the divided consciousness of traumatic sexualization. The result of these efforts signifies, as Ellen Bass and Laura Davis suggest, a process of recovery that is truly characterized by "the courage to heal."[1]

For the majority of women who participated in this research, the recovery process has been arduous, as survivors contend with the original trauma of abuse as well as the on-going threat of revictimization which informs their lives. In some cases, respondents were forced to stop their education or to leave employment in order to recover from the overwhelming feelings and emotions that accompany the process of integration. In other cases, respondents survived by delving deeper into their studies or their work, hoping to find a refuge from the constant pain that threatened to consume their lives. As this research and other studies point out, the healing process varies with the individual; and some victimized daughters recover more fully than others. Recognizing that survivors choose different means to resolve the trauma of incest, Christine Dinsmore characterizes healing as a developmental process:

> Some survivors confront their perpetrators, others do not. Some survivors have bonded with their mothers, others have not. Some survivors remain in the same towns as their families, others move clear across the continent to get away from their families. . . . Regardless of the specific steps, the recovery pattern is a developmental process that includes introspection, such as acknowledging the abuse and working through intense emotions, followed by an action, such as renegotiating family patterns or involvement in a survivor's mission.[2]

Consistent with the developmental perspective, this concluding chapter will elaborate the types of changes that survivors undergo as they seek to find meaning in their lives and value in a female identity. The aspects of recovery that are discussed below represent different phases of the healing process as they have been described by the respondents. While this chapter presents various stages that are associated with recovery, not everyone in the sample experienced all of these changes. Indeed, the majority of survivors were still actively working to resolve the trauma of incest throughout the course of the research.

Beginning with the deconstruction of the idealized father, this chapter will examine the daughter's struggle to separate from the perpetrator and to transform her identification with the aggressor. Reclaiming the sexual self and validating the female persona are among those transformations that will be explored as survivors move toward the reconstruction of the fragmented female self.

Deconstructing the Idealized Father

In both naming and acknowledging the reality of sexual abuse, victimized daughters suffer the loss of the idealized parent as well as a longed-for childhood.[3] Each time the daughter speaks of her traumatization, whether to a therapist, a friend, or a researcher, she affirms the truth of her victimization. Such affirmation involves a painful dismantling of ego defenses that underlie the idealization of the perpetrator. For many survivors, this shift in consciousness is a devastating first step toward recovery, as the daughter attempts to integrate the reality of the incestuous father with the ideal parent in whom she still believes. Here, a twenty-five-year-old, Latina respondent, assaulted in early childhood, describes the agony of coming to terms with the truth about her abusive father:

> Right after I started having flashbacks, I went through a lot of different reactions. It went back and forth between denial and acceptance. How could he? He loved me. He was the only one who loved me. And I started having more flashbacks and I knew it was true and then I hated him. I loved him and I hated him. And in my head I was screaming, "How could you do this to me? You were the only one who loved me!" And it was just the wrong kind of love. Maybe it was not love at all.

As this account suggests, the acknowledgment of the trauma of incest destroys the psychological foundation upon which the child has constructed her sense of reality and her sense of self in relation to the idealized father. Thus, she may vacillate between the pain of acceptance and the safety of denial as she pieces together the memories of a broken and shattered childhood. In this transition from repression to memory recall, the idealization that has facilitated the psychological survival of the abused child is not easily relinquished. As such, many survivors seek to reassure themselves that the trauma of incest is real, that the father in whom they placed their love and trust is also the father who betrayed them. One white respondent explained her feelings of confusion:

> I want to go home but I'm afraid to go home. In therapy I'm looking at patterns. Intellectually, I know this, this, and this about my life. Sometimes I think I must be crazy. If someone asked me what my childhood was like, I used to say and believe it was a good childhood, whatever that means. Now I am so confused I don't know anymore. I sometimes feel I need to go and see my parents. I think I'm making this up. My childhood wasn't that bad. My father couldn't have done all those terrible things.

In a similar response to the realization of incest, another respondent sought to reassure herself that the father she had idealized was in fact the victimizer of her nightmares:

> It's hard for me right now because I don't feel healthy. There's just too much stress. I'm going home for spring break and maybe I'll see him [father] one day. It will be interesting to see. It's like every once in awhile you have to go back and make sure that it's really as bad as you thought it was.

In deconstructing the idealized parent, the daughter may alternate between feelings of rage and feelings of sympathy for the perpetrator with whom she shares an empathic bond.[4] As she seeks to integrate the reality of the abusive father, she may simultaneously search for explanations that preserve his idealized image. In some cases, this conflicting set of needs will result in mother-blaming:

> I was angry at my mother for not standing up for herself, for not standing up for me. She was all tied up in herself and she was tied up in my dad and she was constantly trying to get attention that was not there. Like she whined all the time, pleading with him to talk to her. She would take him into the living room and sit down with him and then she would talk at him because he wouldn't respond. He would not say anything. He would just sit there like this is the most boring and stupidest thing I have ever done. I remember watching this and feeling mad at my mom for putting my father through this. He hated that and I felt sorry for him and I didn't blame him for not wanting to be with her.

For other survivors, the loss of the idealized parent may be informed by race, ethnicity, or religious background. Here the daughter may seek to explain the father's violence as a response to social forces such as racism and antisemitism rather than as a consequence of family conflict. In one such case, a Jewish survivor, forty years of age, discussed the memories of a violent assault by an incestuous stepfather. In recognizing the sadism and cruelty of this abusive parent, the respondent sought to explain his violence in connection with antisemitism:

> After I accepted that this really happened to me and he was capable of doing what I had remembered, I started thinking about what his life might have been like, what could have led him to such cruelty. I read about the pogroms—he had immigrated from Eastern Europe when he was a little boy and I thought about what he might have experienced before he left Eastern Europe and how terrifying it must have been to come here by himself as a young child. During this period of time, I was doing a lot of reading about Jewish identity and I came across a poem that described the massacres in Russia. I remember reading this poem and I just started to cry. This poem was about Jewish men hiding under tables and

behind doors as they helplessly watched the rape of their wives and daughters. I cried because I imagined my stepfather as a little boy, witnessing atrocities that he then reenacted with me. I have no idea if this is true or not. I only imagined this because I guess I needed to believe that he was not totally evil of his own making.

A Catholic survivor, whose incestuous father had once been a priest, offered a somewhat different perspective, explaining the perpetrator's behavior as a result of the guilt and shame she imagined he experienced because of his sexuality:

> Sometimes I just think, poor guy, no wonder he died. He was such a tortured soul. I really think he probably was sexually abused. . . . I think he sort of had a very ambiguous sexual identity himself, and probably could have engaged in homosexual behavior when he was a priest, because that's so common, and felt a lot of guilt and shame for that.

There is in both of these accounts, a desire to understand the perpetrator as well as to preserve some aspect of the ideal parent in whom the abused child can still believe. Further, these two accounts demonstrate the strength of the empathic attachment between victim and abuser as the daughter identifies with the perceived victimization of the aggressor whom she now must acknowledge as real.

Empathy and Separation from the Perpetrator

With the disclosure of incest memories, empathic attachment may also inform confrontations with those fathers who remain present in the lives of survivors. In two such accounts reported here, the abusive father sought sympathy from the respondent. In the first case, the perpetrator admitted that he had been incestuous with his daughter, asking her to understand that his life had been painful too:

Since the abuse stuff has come out, he has been saying things like, you don't know how much this has hurt me and I'm hurting too, and even though this has hurt you, I'm really going through hell around this. He was really trying to make me feel sorry for him like he always did. . . . Most recently we had a confrontation where I finally stood my ground. I was able to say, "Yes, I'm angry with you. I can't believe you did this to me."

In the second case, the father denied having sexually abused the respondent, although he acknowledged that he had not been a good parent:

I said, "Dad, we were always terrified of you, why didn't you ever do anything nice for us?" He said, he was sorry and if he could change he would. He was a terrible father and now he wants a family so I do feel sorry for him. There was one thing that made me swear he was going to admit it right on the phone. He said, "Well, your mom was always hiding behind the Bible and so I guess I just. . ." I swear thought he was going to say, "I came to you." I was shaking. Then he said, "So I guess I had some rage about that." I said, "I know this happened. I know this is the truth." And he said, "No that couldn't have happened. You couldn't have remembered that."

Because the emotional vulnerability of the daughter continues to be exploited by the perpetrator, disengagement from the father is not easily achieved. For many of the women in this study, empathy and anger created conflicting emotional states as feelings of guilt accompanied the desire for separation. Accordingly, a thirty-two-year-old, white, middle-class respondent described her conflicts over establishing autonomy from her parents, and especially her abusive father:

Every time I see them they say, when can you come back, we want to see you so much, even to the point that last week my dad called and said that if I wanted to come up that weekend they would cancel their camping plans because they really wanted to be with me and have all this connection and I got angry. I said, "Don't do that, don't plan your life around me." . . . But at any rate I realized I was feeling guilty again and I needed to call them back and say, "Okay, I can see you this time and that's it and don't ask any more and I'm sorry if that hurts you but this is the way it has to be for me." So I'm learning to be honest with myself and the limits are there so that I don't feel I get out of control.

Another survivor, from a working-class, Latina family, expressed similar ambivalence in choosing not to see her father:

My brothers always say Dad's healthy. They say you should be try-ing to see him and he's your father and you should give him another chance. And I say, "Another chance at what?" And yet I think it would be nice to have a relationship with my father so I question if I'm doing the right thing, or should I try to connect with him again.

The difficulty with which separation is obtained indicates the extent to which incest entraps the child in an emotional rela-tionship that remains viable even after the sexual abuse has stopped. This attachment may be further complicated by the daughter's identification with the perpetrator as a role model for achievement, particularly if her self-worth is tied to accomplish-ments associated with the aggressor. An example is that of a white, thirty-five-year-old graduate student whose studies reflect the interest and endeavors of her incestuous father:

In a lot of ways I've thought my academic journey and my ques-tions are a carryover. In fact I at one time expressed it as a burden that I took on as his unfinished business. You know he had always been questing for self-knowledge or understanding throughout his life, and aborted that journey, or somehow that process did not come to culmination and he died. . . . I tried to see what was his journey and what is mine for my own needs. But I think they are interwoven.

In completing her graduate degree in an area of study that paralleled her father's life and intellectual interests, this respondent chose to follow the path of the aggressor. As her education proceeded along with her recovery process, she increasingly assumed a feminist perspective on her studies and thus was able to retain that which she valued in the perpetrator while making her accomplishments distinctly her own.

This case, in particular, points out the complex nature of victimization in that the identification with the abusive father, which becomes a strategy for psychological survival, is an adaptation to sexual trauma that may simultaneously erode the female self while contributing to the development of an idealized persona. Relinquishing the ideal of the father is therefore confounded by the internalization of the idealized parent, an introjection that has provided a motivation for achievement and the foundation for the daughter's self-esteem. Reclaiming the female self through the deconstruction of the idealized father thus involves transforming the identification with the aggressor while recognizing the sense of self which has been constructed around the ideal of maleness embodied in the perpetrator.

The Identification of the Self as Victim

The recovery of incest trauma forces the realization that the incestuous father is both the idealized male of patriarchal culture as well as the feared parent who has violated the survivor. In acknowledging the true nature of her father's violence, the daughter must also come to terms with the true nature of her victimization. This acknowledgment gives way to the devastating but undeniable reality of the victim self. The loss of the idealized

parent therefore is also the loss of the idealized self, as the survivor begins to integrate the lost memories of her childhood
abuse. During this stage of recovery, identification with suffering
and other forms of victimization may become more pronounced.
As such, respondents spoke of cultural images that reflected a
self-conscious awareness of their victim identity. Among the
most compelling of these images was that of the crucified Christ.
Perhaps because of the sheer pathos and brutality of this religious
symbol, a number of survivors, Christian as well as nonChristian
in background, spoke of the impact of this imagery on their consciousness as they recalled the memories of their abusive
childhoods. In remembering the rape of her four-year-old body, a
thirty-five-year-old respondent offered this insight into her identification with the symbol of the suffering Christ figure:

> I was on vacation and I walked into this church in California and
> suddenly I was transfixed by the image of Christ on the cross. I just
> stared and then I started to cry. Here was this religious symbol that
> had no real meaning for me—I'm Jewish—and I felt all this emo-
> tion. It was the way his body looked, tied to the cross and helpless.
> That was me, the image of my raped body. Only I had been a
> young child and here was this adult male, a god, tapping into my
> unconscious memory. I just cried and cried and I understood why
> Jesus was such a powerful symbol for the oppressed. I really under-
> stood for the first time.

Other religious and cultural symbol systems also offer an identification with victimization. Among these, the myth of Leda
and the Swan represents a cultural affirmation of the sexual vulnerability of the female child. As such myths are immortalized in
poetry and legend, they provide a symbol system through which
the victimized daughter recognizes her own suffering and loss. In
particular, the poetry of Yeats captures the sense of violation that
the mythical Leda endures when she is overcome by the powerful god Zeus who, in the guise of a swan, rapes the young girl:

A sudden blow; the great wings beating still
Above the staggering girl, her thighs caressed
By the dark webs, her nape caught in his bill,
He holds the helpless breast upon his breast

How can those terrified vague fingers push
The feathered glory from her loosening thighs?
And how can body, laid in that white rush,
But feel the strange heart beating where it lies?

A shudder in the loins engenders there
The broken wall, the burning roof and tower
And Agamemnon dead.
                              Being so caught up,
So mastered by the brute blood of the air,
Did she put on his knowledge with his power
Before the indifferent beak could let her drop?[5]

Symbolic representations such as the myth of Leda and the Swan, as well as the crucifixion, externalize the private suffering of the victimized daughter who may only begin to consciously identify with these images once the repressed memories of traumatic sexualization are recalled. Many of the respondents reported that prior to recovery they would readily acknowledge the pain of others, while minimizing or denying their own anguish and distress. Thus, one respondent spoke of the connection between repressed incest trauma and her desire to save the world:

> I think it's also this connection that I feel for wanting to save the world, wanting to help others, and wanting to help people who don't have any power, and wanting to fight for people, do something for people.

As the conscious integration of a victim identity becomes part of the transformative process, the survivor comes to understand that her identification with other powerless members of society has been informed by her own history of abuse. A white, middle-class college student gave this interpretation of her political activism:

> I always felt things really passionately. It's in my activism today. I get really interested and enveloped in my feeling about how wrong it is to abuse women, how wrong slavery is, and why apartheid is so terrible. What I am working on now is trying to realize how I've been a victim and a survivor and to identify with myself instead of everyone else.

Further, the acknowledgment of the survivor's childhood trauma contributes to the erosion of the "bad self" that has been at the core of her development, particularly as experiences of revictimization are reconstructed within the framework of a new self-awareness. Accordingly, respondents often sought reassurance that they were not responsible for the violations and humiliations that they had suffered in the past. For example, one young woman ended her interview with this account of date rape:

> I think I got raped twice when I was in high school, but I've never known for sure because I didn't fight really hard. I said no and they did it anyway. Then I didn't know it was rape. I thought I was having sex. Now I know it's still rape even though I didn't fight to stop it.

The recognition of past victimization, integrated within the context of the original sexual trauma, provides the survivor with a new cognitive structure that contributes to the reconstruction of the self. A manifestation of this transformation is an increased ability to establish and maintain boundaries in those relationships that are potentially victimizing. A nineteen-year-old, African American student explained this shift in consciousness in the following way:

> There are times when I really do say no to guys and they do it anyway. But now I finally made the connection that I have to get up

and leave. It takes a lot for me sometimes. I had this dream and that was the way I finally got away from this guy. I kept saying no and he kept doing stuff to me so I finally got up and left. In the morning I told my friend, "That's how you really just say no. You get up and leave." She says, "Yeah, that's what you do."

Reclaiming the Sexual Self

The deconstruction of the idealized perpetrator allows for the development of a distinct and separate sense of self. As the survivor moves toward a disengagement from the abusive father, sexual intimacy may assume a significant role in the reconstruction of the female persona. Among the women in this study, responses to sexuality varied as some women withdrew from sexual intimacy while others were tentatively engaging in relationships through which they hoped to restructure their sexual responsiveness. The choice to withdraw from intimacy was most frequently reported by survivors in the early stages of recovery when sexuality itself was experienced as threatening and retraumatizing. One bisexual respondent described this aspect of her changing definition of self:

> I was identifying myself as an incest victim and really feeling it. I had been thinking about shaving my head for awhile. I just didn't want to look normal any more. I didn't want people to assume anything. I didn't want to be pretty any more. All last summer I wore big shirts and I didn't accentuate my body at all and I didn't want to be in the beautiful realm any more. I didn't want to be cute. I didn't want anyone looking at me sexually that way. I wanted to look harsh. That's why I am shaving my head.

This account highlights a stage of transformation in which the survivor rejects the definition of herself as sexual object. Her shaved head becomes the symbol of the desexualized and unobjectified self, an alteration in appearance that represents her wish to be safe and to separate from her identity as the sexualized child. This nonconformist presentation of self also draws attention to difference, externalizing the inner sense of violation that the survivor carries with her from the trauma of sexualization.

A heterosexual respondent offered this perspective on transforming her sexualized identity:

> Right after I started remembering, I wasn't attracted to men any more. I wanted to just throw up. If a man looked at me in any kind of sexual way, I just wanted to throw up. Now [a year later] it doesn't bother me much, but I don't really feel anything. I'm not getting any validation from observing how men react to me. And it used to make me feel good. That's how I maintained my self-esteem over all these years. I didn't really feel good about school work. I didn't feel good about what I was doing. I didn't feel really good about myself. And starting last semester, I started feeling good about something within myself, my writing and different things that I have been doing. . . . You can float from one guy to the next for a lifetime, it wouldn't really make you feel any better. Having sexual encounters with men doesn't make you a better person, no, it really doesn't. I don't want validation from them any more.

In searching out alternatives to withdrawal from intimacy, other survivors seek to transform the sexual self within relationships. This aspect of change and reclamation is often difficult to achieve because of the nature of the trauma and its impact on the daughter's developing sexuality. As the survivor seeks to develop new and healthy intimate relationships, intrusive images, flashbacks to the trauma, and feelings of shame and humiliation remain the legacy of incestuous assault. The expression of sexuality therefore becomes the arena in which the survivor may feel she is truly fighting to reclaim her self; for it is here, in the realm of the senses, where the evidence of what Shengold has termed "soul murder" becomes most apparent,[6] as the daughter struggles to discover a sexual intimacy that is not defined by past trauma or by her attachment to the perpetrator. As such, Judith Herman concludes:

> Sexual intimacy presents a particular barrier for survivors of sexual trauma. The physiological processes of arousal and orgasm may be compromised by intrusive traumatic memories; sexual feelings and fantasies may be similarly invaded by reminders of the trauma. Reclaiming one's own capacity for sexual pleasure is a complicated matter; working it out with a partner is more complicated still.[7]

The complications to which Herman refers are evident in the account of a young woman, twenty-one years of age, who was abused by both her father and her brother:

> When I started realizing the abuse, it was in my face always. I've been seeing my brother's face when I've had sex or I will have sex with my boyfriend and be really present and then later in the day I'll see us making love and it will look pornographic to me. So I'm really having to work with that now. My partner has been to a survivor's workshop with Laura Davis and he and I have written down what's okay and what's not okay, what's sometimes okay and what's never okay. We've got a whole list of stuff and it's been very hard on him. . . . I have to be sure when we are having sex that my eyes are open, that I feel I'm with him, that it is us, and it is usually when we're in the shower or something, not in the bedroom. For me having sex in the bedroom, in the missionary position means I will start to check out.

Another respondent, thirty-two years of age, similarly describes her efforts to stay present when she is being sexually intimate:

> I was very unconnected with my body. If someone were to hug me, I just dissociated. It wasn't until a couple of years ago that I started feeling sexual feelings from someone who touched my breasts, for example. Before, someone might touch my breasts and there was nothing there. It didn't affect me. Now, if I'm making love with someone, I have to say, he's holding me, he's touching me, this is

happening. You can respond to this. It's like trying to keep in my body when this is going on.

In addition to controlling dissociative responses and the problem of intrusive flashbacks, the restructuring or elimination of sexual fantasies represents another shift in consciousness that signifies a disengagement from the perpetrator. As in the other areas of sexuality, respondents report intentional and concentrated efforts to transform sexual interaction. In the case of fantasy, survivors report the desire to eliminate themes of sadomasochism and domination from their sexual imagination. In one case, a thirty-six-year-old respondent reported:

> I just won't allow myself to think about being dominated any more, or punished, even in fantasy. I could always have orgasms with my lover if I imagined that she was controlling me in some way and now I just stop the thoughts as soon as they appear. And before I make love, I tell myself, no fantasies, even if that means less intensity. I really feel better after making love now. There is no residual shame or guilt.

Another survivor offers this account of her efforts to eliminate rape and sexual violence from her fantasies:

> I don't think we are born with our sexuality that way. I knew I had to start from a place of not feeling guilty about the fantasies in the same way I stopped feeling quilty about the incest. They were both coming from the same place. Letting go of the guilt was really important. But I wanted to take it further than that. I wanted to stop having them. . . .
>
> It helped for me to feel that I *deserved* to have passionate feelings, and that they didn't have to be linked to those fantasies. I came to the point where I really understood that they weren't *my* fantasies. They'd been imposed on me through the abuse. And gradually, I began to be able to have orgasms without thinking about the SM [sadomasochism], without picturing my father doing something to me.

Once I separated the fantasy from the feeling, I'd consciously impose other powerful images on the feeling—like seeing a waterfall. If they can put SM on you, you can put waterfalls there instead. I reprogrammed myself. Instead of having to say "I'll do anything you want," I would see a waterfall and have the same intensity of feeling.[8]

When such transformations are realized, survivors express gratitude for the sexuality they can now claim as their own, as the following quote reveals:

I used to have these weird feelings about being spanked and it would turn me on. Right now it's better. I don't feel I'm having gross fantasies that are degrading or humiliating. Anytime I feel sexual I am so happy, I just say thank you.

For other victimized daughters, reclaiming the sexual self involves avoiding intimate attachments that replicate the bonds to the father/perpetrator. In this regard, respondents report ending abusive relationships while making a conscious effort to develop new forms of intimacy that are not characterized by the socio-emotional conditioning of traumatic sexualization. A case in point is that of a twenty-one-year-old survivor from a working-class family who reported the following:

I can say almost all my relationships have been secret except for one lover that I had by choice. That's what I call him, my choice, my first love by choice. So I've always had these real secret relationships with men that are way older. This guy now is thirty-nine. I just want to stop that. No more secrets. It just makes me feel too bad.

Disengaging from the Internalized Aggressor

The reconstruction of the survivor's sexuality represents a significant move towards autonomy from the perpetrator and from

151

the definition of self as body. Equally significant are those transformations that involve relinquishing the identification with the abuser as this connection is manifested in the internalized aggressor.[9] Such changes begin with an awareness of the behavioral aspects of this identification and the desire to alter behavior that is aggressive and harmful toward others. One white, middle-class survivor, for example, spoke of violent behavior that replicated the aggression of her abusive father:

> I've had my cat for nine years and I treated her the same way my father treated us, and the same way he treated our dog, too. I was very restrictive, very controlling, yelled and screamed. I've hit her a lot. I've picked her up and thrown her. I've wanted to get rid of her. I tried to get rid of her a lot. . . . Now I have this really loving relationship with her and I really see her as a teacher because I've learned so much from her and how I've related to her. And I've been so happy that I've learned this with a cat and not with a child.

A teenage mother expressed similar fears around the possibility of her own abusive behavior:

> It's really bad. I don't know how to let the anger go. I know I should learn to release that anger because you could really hurt someone and then you might get the baby taken away from you. Sometimes I'm afraid I won't be able to control myself. I spoke to Mom about it and she says she will help me be a good mother.

In one final example of disengagement from the aggressor, a respondent described her commitment to change following a battering incident with her partner that revealed the extent to which she had internalized the abuser:

> I was so angry. I don't even know what it was but I hit her and it was really scary for me because I thought I was out of control and I didn't want that to happen. . . . And then when I hit her, I thought, "Oh, my God, it really has changed and I can't do this

ever again." I swore I would never hit anyone again. If I have to hit someone, I'm going to hit a punching bag. I'm going to go running.

Once the idealization of the perpetrator is diminished, the daughter may see within herself the hated aggressor of her childhood and, as the respondents cited above, she may act to change that which is a source of self-hatred and condemnation. In transforming the internalized aggressor, a validation of the female persona emerges through the daughter's recognition of the child self with whom she can now empathize. Shifting empathic understanding from the perpetrator to the self represents an important step toward healing, one that is decribed by a respondent as a significant turning point in her life:

I think the first time it really started was when I was separated from my husband and feeling lonely and very scared about whether I could make it through graduate school. My mother, for some reason, sent me a picture of myself as a little girl and it was the best thing she could have done because I remember sitting in my living room—I had a rocking chair and boxes around me and my books and this picture popped up on the books and I looked at that little girl and I said, "Wow, she's really something." It was like I wasn't looking at myself and I thought, this little girl looks so happy and innocent and a neat kid. I thought she really deserves a good life. . . . It really was the first time I had a gentle sense about myself. It was like the first emotional connection with myself, that I was worthwhile.

Self-Validation and the Reconnection to the Female Persona

The integration of the trauma of sexual abuse can lead to the dismantling of the false self that has been constructed through the victimized daughter's identification with the perpetrator. As described by the respondents in this study, the process of change involves both the acknowledgment of the victimized child self and of a female identity that can be valued and trusted. For many women, this shift in self-identification begins to occur in the therapeutic setting where, through the process of transference, the survivor recreates a childlike dependency on the therapist who replaces the idealized parent in the unconscious of the survivor.[10] When this transference is negotiated successfully by the therapist, the clinical relationship becomes a model of respectful caretaking through which the survivor's autonomy may be safely tested and realized.

The attachment to the therapist, in replicating the bonds of childhood, provides an interactive framework for validating the denigrated and rejected female self. In this regard, the gender of the therapist has bearing on the reconstructive process in that a female therapist signifies a crucial primary attachment through which gender validation is obtained. This aspect of clinical treatment is especially important because of the destructive effects of incest on the mother-daughter bond. In developing a supportive therapeutic relationship, survivors can establish a framework for reconnecting with the rejected mother and thus with the female self that has been denied.

This stage of recovery often involves a growing awareness on the part of the survivor that her mother has also been a victim, a realization that provides a foundation for establishing an empathic connection which had been lost between mother and child. In some cases the mother may facilitate the development of an empathic bond through the acknowledgment of the daughter's abuse and through her efforts to separate from the perpetrator. The following account from a twenty-seven-year-old survivor will help to illustrate this shift in the mother-daughter relationship and the lessening of mother blame among survivors:

I used to have a lot of anger and hatred and disgust toward my mother. Now she's my best friend. It began to change when she finally left my abusive father. She lived in a state of denial for a long time. She's very good at denial. This is a woman who got beat twice a week and said there was no abuse in her relationship. When she left him, it was that year when she was just emotionally jello. She would call me everyday and cry on the phone. . . . She desperately clung to me because I was the only person who would listen to her, the only person that maybe could see that my father was a horrible person because nobody else saw that. So it was like this validation happened. And she's wonderful now. She's real invested in working through it and admitting that it happened. She can say things like, "I was a battered wife for twenty-five years."

In a similar report, another respondent, twenty-three years of age, described her changing attitude toward her mother following her separation from the perpetrator:

I was mad at my mom for a long time. I wished she would have stood up for herself and taken care of herself and made herself healthy. My main anger was watching her grovel at my dad's feet. Now, she's great. She's healthy. She's got the same attitude that I do towards my dad, that basically you cannot hold out hope for this man because if you do you are going to make yourself nuts. And I told her that I wished she had paid more attention to me, especially after I got back from the trip where my father had abused me. I said I wanted her to take his picture and write pervert under it and plaster it all over the clinic where he works so that everyone would know what this great doctor did to his daughter. She agreed with me. She said she was glad I was in therapy getting help. It's like for twenty-five years she's been asleep. She's a different person now. Her real person was completely buried and now it's come out again and that's good.

Even among those survivors whose mothers had not severed their emotional attachment to the perpetrator, respondents reported empathizing with their plights as abused wives and as daughters who themselves had been victimized but who remained in denial. A case in point is that of a thirty-five-year-old woman who spoke of her mother's painful childhood:

I think my mother was abused as a child. She of course denies everything. She is the oldest. Her parents were poor farmers and she left home to live with this older couple who were childless and needed someone to help around the house when she was about thirteen. When I asked her why she left home she insists it was because financially they were just having a hard time and these people offered her a chance to go to school. . . . So she left home and my sense of it, and I've asked her a lot of questions, is that she was in some form abused. Here's this mother having babies every year with this poor father. I just assumed probably she'd been sexually abused. I don't know. She denies any memory of anything like that.

It may also be the case that the empathy the daughter develops for the mother is not reciprocated. Under those circumstances, the daughter may seek to emotionally disengage from the non-supportive mother. In asserting the need for emotional distance, one adult survivor offered this perspective:

My mother wants me to tell her more about what I found out about the incest but every time she asks, it's always under the guise of, you tell me what happened and I'll redefine it for you and so I just won't talk to her about it. . . . In fact, we had it out when I first came back to town a couple of months ago. . . . It escalated to the point where I just said, "I'm not having this conversation" and I walked out because she said, "I don't think you understand. I think what you remember isn't correct and isn't what happened and I want to tell you what happened to you," and I just said, "no." I walked out and about thirty minutes later I went back and I said, "Look, I know you want to be innocent about this but you don't have control over this situation. I am a different person from you and I experienced these things," and I tried to assert the difference. . . . I think she's had an enormous difficulty separating from me and so it was nice to be able to pull back and assert that. I think right now what I'm doing is trying to keep the separation.

Other adult respondents sought to explain the mother's lack of empathy as a consequence of generational violence:

She's not like a bad person or anything. When I was little she was a good person to me and now she won't take care of me. She's the mom, you know. . . . When I told her about the abuse she at first said she was not surprised. Then she called me back the next night and asked, "What kind of proof do you have? I can't really support you unless you have some proof." She wasn't going to support me at all. She wrote me this letter. It was so gross. She writes, "I've shared with your father your accusations against him and we've decided to deal with it together. You can either let this make you bitter for the rest of your life or you can bury it under the blood of Jesus like I have." My mom has this sense that my dad would be a normal person if we could just help him, if he would feel better about himself. I think her dad was a massive batterer and I'm sure she was abused. I think her father tried to kill my grandmother, rigged some weird thing up in the attic. I think he was strange. It all passes down.

This respondent was among those women who, in separating from their mothers, turned to spirituality and especially goddess symbolism to validate the female self:

The whole idea of the goddess changed my life. No more god any-more; female power, it's here, out there. I don't really believe there is a god anymore and I don't believe there's hell. I really want to do something because I feel so much more powerful in my life.

The identification with female spiritual power has been vari-ously construed in the contemporary feminist movement.[11] The value of such identification for incest survivors from diverse backgrounds would seem to bear directly on the loss of the female self and the rupture of the mother-daughter bond. Thus, a number of women, including African American, Latina, and white survivors have turned to female spirituality in the process of healing from an abusive childhood. As one woman said, "I wanted it to be like Demeter and Persephone, the mother who saves the daughter, but it wasn't anything like that." In the

157

absence of real maternal strength and effectuality, feminist theology and ritual offer a connection to a powerful female symbol that can validate the female self. Francis Wesley, in fact, suggests that attachment to religious symbols replicates the process of therapeutic transference in that representations of the divine signify the idealized mother in the unconscious of the individual.[12] The work of Kathie Carlson supports this interpretation. In her research on female archetypes and the mother-daughter relationship, she concludes:

> For a growing child or adult woman to experience herself as being in the image of the positive elementary mother is, on the human level, a pleasurable and reassuring experience. For this to be experienced on the level of the Goddess, to be "just like *Her*," conveys a profound sense of meaning and value to one's life and one's womanhood; it may even take on mystical proportions.[13]

Accordingly, research on feminist healing rituals has found that abused women tend to envision the goddess both as mother and as self.[14] In one such case of creative visualization, a woman reported:

> The first image was my mother or someone very much like her. It wasn't anything like a Greek goddess, that just didn't have reality for me. What I was, was someone earthy with lots of varied experience and human expressions. In the second confrontation, I imagined myself more as myself, but larger than life.[15]

In those cases where the mother-daughter bond cannot be reestablished, the engagement in female spirituality provides a context for reconstructing the ideal mother and in so doing, reclaiming the valued feminine persona.

Participation in feminist rituals, as described by the respondents, represents a creative approach to recovery that augments the therapeutic process. One respondent, twenty-one years of age, created a ritual entitled, "A Mock But Real Memorial

Service For the Death of My Father." She then organized a gathering of her friends where she read the following text that she
had prepared for the ceremony:

> We are gathered here in the cradle of the goddess to mourn the
> death of Toni's father; to mourn the death of an ideal she loved
> with all her heart. We are saddened by the feeling of loss this death
> has caused, but we also know that in death there is rebirth. Rebirth
> in the living. In Toni there is a rebirth of faith in herself and a
> rebirth of love for her body and her spirit. . . . This death is sad, but
> out of this death, like a pheonix I am reborn. I reclaim my soul. I
> reclaim my body. I reclaim my mind. Most importantly, in my
> rebirth, I take back my little girl. I am her caretaker now and I will
> keep her safe.

The engagement in ritualized healing offers insight into the creativity that sustains and empowers the survivor. Such approaches
to the resolution of incest trauma are also evident in a broad
range of other creative endeavors, including the production of
art, poetry, and drama.

The Creative Imagination and the Reintegrated Self

The study of the relationship between creativity and victimization is a compelling area of research. Alice Miller, in
particular, has studied the relationship between suffering and creativity, focusing on the life and work of the writer Franz Kafka.[16]
Like Kafka, Maya Angelou represents another outstanding literary figure whose work reveals a connection between artistic
endeavor and personal suffering. As discussed in the earlier chapter on empathic attachment, Angelou's autobiography addresses
the effects of sexual abuse on the developing child, revealing the
way in which sexual assault deprives the young Maya of speech
and a belief in herself. In *I Know Why the Caged Bird Sings*,

Angelou writes the victimized child into being and thus restores her voice through the retelling of the trauma of sexualization.

More recently, the biographers of the poet Anne Sexton, and the writer Virginia Woolf, have interpreted the creative lives of these two literary figures through the lens of sexual abuse.[17] In reading the poetry of Sexton, one is struck by allusions to incest that inform her prose, as the images she creates appear to be fragmented memories of fear and victimization. In the riveting poem, "Briar Rose (Sleeping Beauty)" she names the tormenter of her sleep:

> There was a theft.
> That much I am told.
> I was abondoned,
> That much I know.
> I was forced backward.
> I was forced forward.
> I was passed hand to hand
> like a bowl of fruit.
> Each night I am nailed into place
> and I forget who I am.
> Daddy?
> That's another kind of prison.
> It's not the prince at all,
> but my father
> drunkenly bent over my bed,
> circling the abyss like a shark,
> my father thick upon me
> like some sleeping jellyfish.
> What voyage this, little girl?
> This coming out of prison?
> God help—
> this life after death?[18]

Although the exact nature of Sexton's victimization is still unclear, her biographer, Diane Middlebrook, offers convincing evidence that she was indeed an abused daughter whose poetry provided insight into the tormented woman who would ultimately commit suicide. Thus, for artists such as Woolf and Sexton, their creativity could not save them as each, in the end, chose death over life.

Like Sexton and Woolf, it is not uncommon for survivors to reveal their hidden childhoods through acts of artistic and intellectual creation that help to break the silence of their victimization and end their isolation. For example, the groundbreaking anthologies, *Voices in the Night: Women Speaking About Incest* and *I Never Told Anyone: Writings By Women Survivors of Child Sexual Abuse*[19] represent published collections in which survivors tell their stories through a range of literary styles and prose. Among the many moving contributions in these works, is the recollection entitled "Black Girl Learn the Holiness of Motherhood," in which the author, Susan Chute, reconstructs the trauma of victimization through the power and imagery of words. In this excerpt, she describes attending the funeral of a white woman at which her father, a black preacher, gave the eulogy:

> Daddy up there at the pulpit talkin now, bout the good person the white woman wuz, now gone to bliss in heaven & streets & castles made a solid gold. Willa recall when she ask about that, her daddy open his mouth & show her his golden teeth, sayin it wuz god's personal gift to him, and god spoke to him through the gold in his mouth, and that wuz how he preach. She member how many times she touch those teeth wid her tongue an it felt smooth & cold & bitter. She fraid god gonna talk wid her tongue coverin the gold sometime, an daddy not gonna know what god is sayin to him.
>
> Her daddy up there still preachin but Willa not lissnin now. She watchin a spaghetti sauce stain on daddy's suit, thinkin, "It the same color as the first nite when he touch me & the blood trickle & he call it the RED SEA OF MOSES & say god be very pleased cos we wuz lovin people."[20]

Writings such as Chute's facilitate the healing process through an affirmation of the realities that govern women's lives. Accordingly, the editors of *Voices in the Night* believe that creative expression provides a framework in which to gain control over the trauma of incest:

> We conceived of this collection out of our own sense of the empowering force of writing out our worst feelings and fantasies. Bringing them out of the shadows began to get them to a manageable size. . . . Since we as editors are passionately convinced of the necessity and excitement of rendering women's lives into art as healing, enriching and affirmative experiences, there is little or no dialogue possible with the critic who will attempt to silence us in this way.[21]

Among the women in this study, creative aspects of healing were realized through diverse forms of artistic expression, including poetry, plays, films, paintings, and sculpture. For some respondents, art became the vehicle through which they reconstructed the wounded self. An example of this phenomenon is offered by a twenty-seven-year-old, white, middle-class respondent who spoke of her writing as a source of empowerment:

> I have this novel. I finished it and sent it off to get published. Orginally when I did it, the main character was male. He was a child and he goes through all these things, but there was no resolution. Now I've written it again and the main character is a female, and it's really interesting to see the changes I've made in it and there is resolution. It's full of what is going on inside of me. The writing becomes the body in a way. The space that I'm climbing, claiming your body back from people. It's the intellectual way that I have of reclaiming myself.

This survivor provides an insightful perspective on the reinvention of the female self through the act of writing and creative thought. While her intellectual process allows her to transcend the physicality of her body, the person she becomes in her imagination is the newly created image of herself as woman. No longer identified with a male protagonist, this shift in artistic focus reflects her disengagement from the perpetrator and the internalized male ego ideal of her childhood; and because life sometimes imitates art, she expressed this new vision of the self in her rejection of her former male identification:

> I really wanted to be my brother. I used to steal his clothes and take them to school and put his clothes on. I do that with boyfriends, like wear a lot of their clothes. I used to wear my husband's clothes. I wouldn't buy clothes for myself, I'd just wear his. I don't do that any longer. I have my own clothes now, even underwear. I used to wear his underwear, everything, but not anymore. Now I wear my own.

As creativity is broadly defined, it is significant that a number of teen mothers in the study offered a somewhat different view on the relationship between female creativity and self acceptance, linking affirmation of the female self to biological reproduction rather than intellectual and artistic expression. These respondents spoke specifically of their ability to create life and the validation they experienced in the act of childbirth. In giving birth, these young women expressed, perhaps for the first time, a positive connection to their body and to a gendered identity. Here, a twenty-three-year-old respondent from a white, working-class background recalled the birth of her child four years before, a daughter whose adoption she planned while still pregnant:

> I felt so barren, so dry and just like, if sex is all I'm good for, that's fine. When I got pregnant I got a new life. It was like coming out. It changed my life. I learned to take control. I planned the whole adoption. I did it all and it turned out well and it was my accomplishment. I had this beautiful baby. She was so cute, so gorgeous, perfect. I did that. It just changed everything.

Another teen mother, a Latina from a working-class family, considered adoption but chose to raise her child as the pregnancy developed:

> I was set on giving the baby up for adoption until two months before I had her and totally changed my mind. She was living and I knew she was part of me and I could feel this baby inside of me and I wanted to keep her. Having a baby to me was hard, but it was great. I would do it again if I had to. Just to look at the baby and to think I helped this child develop. I created this child and if I have to, I'll do it again.

The teen mothers interviewed for this study tended to place a great deal of hope in the idealized life they imagined for their children. In this regard, they believe they will protect them from the abuse that they themselves had suffered and they fantasize a close and nurturing relationship between mother and child. In a very real sense, the birth of a child for the adolescent mother who has been victimized symbolizes the rebirth of the child self who can now be embraced and nurtured.

Conclusion

The process of change and transformation that is elaborated here highlights the significant developmental issues that influence the personality formation of sexually abused daughters. In as much as incest violates the emotional and physical boundaries of the child, her identification with the violent father begins with the empathic attachment to the perpetrator who comes to represent an ego ideal in the psychological development of the daughter. As she seeks to construct her identity in the image of the aggressor, the personality of the daughter may find its expression in a mind/body split, a fragmentation of the self in which the internalized aggressor signifies male strength and power while the internalized victim represents female weakness and powerlessness. Thus, the trauma of sexualization leads to the development of a divided consciousness wherein the daughter comes to experience herself both as violated body and as the male ego ideal through which she seeks to reinvent herself.

Recovery from traumatic sexualization therefore begins with the process of reintegration whereby the original trauma is brought to consciousness. Only then can the idealization of the perpetrator give way to the reality of his sexual violence. With the deconstruction of the idealized father, the daughter can begin to reclaim and redefine the female self, diminishing the impact of the internalized aggressor. The core identity of the survivor may then be reconstructed as the survivor reclaims the right to her body and to her sexuality. Through the development of attachments that affirm the female self she discovers the sense of value and personal worth that the trauma of incest has taken from her. To this process of reintegration and healing, survivors bring their creativity and belief in themselves.

As the accounts of the respondents so poignantly suggest, this transformation is a difficult and tenuous process, one that involves relinquishing psychological defenses and personality adaptations which facilitated survival under the most untenable of circumstances; and as pointed out earlier, some survivors never achieve the kind of resolution that is described here. Even among those women who recover, the effects of traumatic sexualization may continue to inform their lives, as the emotional scars of sexual abuse remain part of the life experience of the incest survivor. Although change may be painstakingly slow, the accounts of the women in this study illustrate that the reconstruction of the damaged and violated self is possible. Ultimately, the lives of victimized daughters, as revealed through their retrospective life histories, represent significant acts of courage as each respondent has begun to confront the fears of her past and the traumas that have threatened the survival of the self.

Notes

1. Introduction

1. A translation of this myth is found in Rosemary Radford Ruether, *Womanguides: Readings Toward A Feminist Theology* (Boston: Beacon Press, 1985), 44–47.

2. Ibid., 46.

3. See Lee Stroessner Brunngraber, "Father Daughter Incest: Immediate and Long Term Effects of Sexual Abuse," *Advance in Nursing Science* 8, no. 4 (1986): 15–35; David Finkelhor, *Sexually Victimized Children* (New York: The Free Press, 1979); Jean Renvoize, *Incest: A Family Pattern* (New York and London: Routledge, 1982); and Diana E.H. Russell, "The Incidence and Prevalence of Intrafamilial and Extrafamilial Sexual Abuse of Female Children," *Child Abuse and Neglect* 7, no. 2 (1983): 133–46.

4. *The Denver Post*, May 9, 1991.

5. Christine A. Courtois, *Healing the Incest Wound: Adult Survivors in Therapy* (New York: W.W. Norton, 1988); Judith Lewis Herman, *Father-Daughter Incest* (Cambridge, MA: Harvard University Press, 1981); Judith Lewis Herman, *Trauma and Recovery: The Aftermath of Violence—From Domestic Abuse to Political Terror* (New York: Basic Books, 1992); Wendy Maltz and Beverly Holman, *Incest and Sexuality: A Guide to Understanding*

and Healing (Lexington, MA: D.C. Heath, 1987); Karin Meiselman, *Incest: A Psychological Study of Causes and Effects with Treatment Recommendations* (San Francisco: Jossey-Bass, 1978); Karin Meiselman, *Resolving the Trauma of Incest* (San Francisco: Jossey-Bass, 1990); Diana E.H. Russell, *The Secret Trauma: Incest in the Lives of Girls and Women* (New York: Basic Books, 1986).

6. Carolyn I. Thornton and James H. Carter, "Treatment Considerations With Black Incestuous Families," *Journal of the National Medical Association* 78, no. 1 (1986): 49–53.

7. Christine Courtois, *Healing the Incest Wound;* Judith Herman, *Father-Daughter Incest.*

8. See Linda Gordon and Paul O'Keefe, "Incest as a Form of Family Violence: Evidence from Historical Case Records," *Journal of Marriage and Family* 46, no. 1 (1984): 27–34; James W. Selby, Lawrence G. Calhoun, Joanne M. Jones, and Lisolette Matthews, "Families of Incest: A Collation of Clinical Impressions," *International Journal of Social Psychiatry* 26, no. 1 (1980): 7–16; and Donna L. Truesdall, John S. McNeil, and Jeanne P. Deschner, "Incidence of Wife Abuse in Incestuous Families," *Social Work* 31, no. 21 (1986): 138–40.

9. Judith Herman, *Father-Daughter Incest.*

10. See Audrey Droisen, "Racism and Anti-Semitism," in *Child Sexual Abuse: Feminist Perspectives*, Emily Driver and Audrey Droisen, eds. (London: MacMillan Education LTD, 1989), 158–169; Robert Pierce and Lois Pierce, "Child Sexual Abuse: A Black Perspective," in *Violence in the Black Family,* ed. Robert L. Hampton (Lexington, Mass: Lexington Books, 1987), 67–85; and Carolyn Thornton and James Carter, "Treatment Considerations With Black Incestuous Families."

11. Robert Pierce and Lois Pierce, "Child Sexual Abuse: A Black Perspective," 74.

12. Audrey Droisen, "Racism and Anti-Semitism," 163.

13. Sigmund Freud, "The Aetiology of Hysteria," in *Collected Papers,*

Vol. I, trans. Joan Riviere (London: The Hogarth Press, 1949), 185.

14. Ibid., 198–99.

15. Larry Wolff, *Postcards from the End of the World: Child Abuse in Freud's Vienna* (New York: Atheneum, 1988), 205.

16. See Jeffrey Moussaieff Masson, *The Assault on Truth: Freud's Suppression of the Seduction Theory* (New York: Farrar, Straus & Giroux, 1984); Alice Miller, *Thou Shalt Not Be Aware: Society's Betrayal of the Child* (New York: Farrar, Straus & Giroux, 1984); and Florence Rush, *The Best Kept Secret: Sexual Abuse of Children* (Englewood Cliffs, New Jersey: Prentice-Hall, 1980).

17. Jean Goodwin, "Post Traumatic Symptoms in Incest Victims," in *Post Traumatic Stress Disorder in Children*, eds. Spencer Eth and Robert S. Pynoos (Washington, D.C.: American Psychiatric Press, 1985), 157–68.

18. Ibid.

19. Judith Herman, *Trauma and Recovery*, esp. chapter 6; For other research on post traumatic stress syndrome in incest survivors, see Susan V. McCleer, Esther Deblinger, Marc S. Atkins, Edna B. Foa, and Diana L. Ralphe, "Post Traumatic Stress Disorder in Sexually Abused Children," *Journal of the American Academy of Child and Adolescent Psychiatry* 27, no. 5 (1988): 650–54; and Vicky V. Wolfe, Carole Gentell, and David A. Wolfe, "The Impact of Sexual Abuse on Children: A PTSD Formulation," *Behavior Therapy* 20, no. 2 (1989): 215–28.

20. Judith Herman, *Trauma and Recovery*.

21. Nancy Chodorow, *The Reproduction of Mothering: Psychoanalysis and the Sociology of Gender* (Berkeley: University of California Press, 1978); Dorothy Dinnerstein, *The Mermaid and the Minotaur* (New York: Harper and Row, 1976); Jean Baker Miller, *Toward a New Psychology of Women* (Boston: Beacon, 1986); and Juliet Mitchell, *Psychoanalysis and Feminism* (London: Allen Lane, 1974).

22. See, for example, Judith V. Jordan, Alexandra G. Kaplan, Jean Baker Miller, Irene P. Stiver, and Janet L. Surrey, *Women's*

Growth in Connection: Writings from the Stone Center (New York and London: The Guilford Press, 1991).

23. See, for example, Jessica Benjamin, *The Bonds of Love: Psychoanalysis, Feminism, and the Problem of Domination* (New York: Pantheon, 1988); Jane Flax, *Thinking Fragments: Psychoanalysis, Feminism, and Postmodernism in the Contemporary West* (Berkeley: University of California Press, 1990); Shirley Nelson Gardner, Claire Kahane, and Madelon Sprengnether, eds., *The (M)other Tongue: Essays in Feminist Psychoanalytic Interpretation* (Ithaca and London: Cornell University Press, 1985); and Marcia Westkott, *The Feminist Legacy of Karen Horney* (New Haven and London: Yale University Press, 1986).

2. Incest and the Destruction of the Mother-Daughter Bond

1. For a discussion of the role of mothers in personality formation, see Nancy Chodorow, *The Reproduction of Mothering: Psychoanalysis and the Sociology of Gender* (Berkeley: University of California Press, 1978); and Judith V. Jordan, Alexandra G. Kaplan, Jean Baker Miller, Irene P. Stiver, and Janet L. Surrey, *Women's Growth in Connection: Writings from the Stone Center* (New York and London: The Guilford Press, 1991).

2. Judith Lewis Herman, *Father-Daughter Incest* (Cambridge, MA: Harvard University Press, 1981); Judith Lewis Herman and Lisa Hirshman, "Father-Daughter Incest," in Elizabeth Abel and Emily F. Abel, eds., *Signs Reader* (Chicago: University of Chicago Press, 1983) 257–58; Karin Meiselman, *Incest: A Psychological Study of Causes and Effects with Treatment Recommendations* (San Francisco: Jossey-Bass, 1978).

3. Judith Lewis Herman, *Father-Daughter Incest*, 103.

4. Karin Meiselman, *Incest*.

5. Mark D. Everson, Wanda M. Hunter, Desmond K. Runyon, Gail A. Edelsohn, and Martha L. Coulter, "Maternal Support Following Disclosure of Incest," *American Journal of*

Orthopsychiatry 59 (1989), 197–207; Linda Gordon, *Heroes of Their Own Lives: The Politics and History of Family Violence* (New York: Viking Press, 1988); Judith Lewis Herman, *Father-Daughter Incest*; Margaret H. Myer, "A New Look at Mothers of Incest Victims," *Journal of Social Work and Human Sexuality* 3, nos. 2–3 (1984–5): 47–58; Diana E. H. Russell, *The Secret Trauma: Incest in the Lives of Girls and Women* (New York: Basic Books, 1986).

6. Diane Ehrensaft, "When Women and Men Mother," in Joyce Treblicot, ed., *Mothering: Essays in Feminist Theory* (Totowa, NJ: Rowman and Allenheld, 1984), 41–61, esp. 49.

7. Juliet Mitchell, *Women's Estate* (New York: Pantheon, 1971).

8. Ronald Fairbairn, *An Object Relations Theory of the Personality* (New York: Basic Books, 1952); Donald Winnicott, *Collected Papers* (London: Tavistock, 1958); Michael Balint, *Primary Love and Psycho-Analytic Technique* (London: Tavistock, 1965). See also Janet Sayers, *Sexual Contradictions: Psychology, Psychoanalysis, and Feminism* (London: Tavistock, 1986), for a feminist critique of traditional object relations theory.

9. Ronald Fairbairn, *An Object Relations Theory of the Personality*, 11.

10. Ibid., 38–48.

11. Sigmund Freud, "On Narcissism: An Introduction," in *The Standard Edition of the Complete Psychological Works*, Vol. 14 (London: The Hogarth Press, 1958).

12. Donald Winnicott, *Collected Papers*, 50–53.

13. Ibid., 302–06.

14. Janet Sayers, *Sexual Contradictions*, 67.

15. Gayle Rubin, "The Traffic in Women," in Rayna R. Reiter, ed., *Toward an Anthropology of Women* (New York: Monthly Press, 1975), 157–210.

16. Ibid., 202.

17. Nancy Chodorow, "Family Structure and Feminine Personality," in Michelle Rosaldo and Louise Lamphere, eds., *Woman, Culture and Society* (Palo Alto, CA: Stanford University Press, 1974), 43–66.

18. Nancy Chodorow and Susan Contratto, "The Fantasy of the Perfect Mother," in Barrie Thorne, ed., with Marilyn Yalom, *Rethinking the Family: Some Feminist Questions* (New York: Longman, 1980), 54–75, esp. 65.

19. In particular, Chodorow and Contratto discuss the work of Nancy Friday, *My Mother My Self* (New York: Delacorte, 1977); Judith Arcana, *Our Mother's Daughters* (Berkeley: Shameless Hussy Press, 1979); and Dorothy Dinnerstein, *The Mermaid and the Minotaur* (New York: Harper and Row, 1976).

20. Grace B. Hubbard, "Mothers' Perceptions of Incest: Sustained Disruption and Turmoil," *Archives of Psychiatric Nursing* 3, no. 1 (1989): 34–40.

21. Interview with Gayle Quick Huffaker, Denver, CO, March 2, 1993.

22. Miriam M. Johnson, "Fathers, Mothers, and Sex Typing," *Sociological Inquiry* 45 (1975): 15–26; and "Heterosexuality, Male Dominance, and the Father Image," *Sociological Inquiry*, 51, no. 2 (1981): 129–39.

23 Miriam Johnson, "Fathers, Mothers, and Sex Typing," 24.

24. Ann Ferguson, "On Conceiving Motherhood and Sexuality: A Feminist Materialist Approach," in Joyce Treblicot, ed., *Mothering: Essays in Feminist Theory* (Totowa, NJ: Rowman and Allenheld, 1984), 153–67.

25. Ibid., 164.

26. Ibid., 160–61.

27. David Finkelhor, *Sexually Victimized Children* (New York: The Free Press, 1979); Donna L. Truesdall, John S. McNeil, and Jeanne P. Deschner, "Incidence of Wife Abuse in Incestuous Families," *Social Work* 31, no. 21 (1986): 138–40.

28. Paula J. Caplan, *Don't Blame Mother: Mending the Mother-Daughter Relationship* (New York: Harper and Row, 1989).

29. Feminist critiques of mother blame in incest are discussed in Lena Dominelli, "Father-Daughter Incest: Patriarchy's Shameful

Secret," *Critical Social Policy* 6, no. 16 (1986): 8–22; Kerri James and Lauri Mackinnon, "The 'Incestuous Family' Revisited: A Critical Analysis of Family Therapy Myths," *Journal of Marital and Family Therapy* 16, no. 1 (1990): 71–88; Mary MacLeod and Esther Saraga, "Challenging the Orthodoxy: Towards a Feminist Theory and Practice," *Feminist Review* 28 (1988): 16–55; Mary McIntosh, "Introduction to an Issue: Family Secret as Public Drama," *Feminist Review* 28 (1988): 6–15; Kevin McIntyre, "Role of Mothers in Father-Daughter Incest: A Feminist Analysis," *Social Work* 26 (1981): 462–66; and Esther Wattenberg, "In a Different Light: A Feminist Perspective on the Role of Mothers in Father-Daughter Incest," *Child Welfare* 64, no. 3 (1985): 203–11.

30. Karin Meiselman, *Incest,* 112.

31. Noel Lustig, John W. Dresser, Seth W. Spellman, and Thomas A. Murray, "Incest: A Family Group Survival Pattern," *Archives of General Psychiatry* 14 (1966): 31–40; and Naomi G. Rucker and Karen L. Lombardi, "The Familial Menage-a-Trois: Mother-Daughter Sexuality and Father-Daughter Incest," *Journal of Contemporary Psychotherapy* 20, no. 2 (1990): 99–107.

32. Lydia Tinling, "Perpetuation of Incest by Significant Others: Mothers Who Do Not Want to See," *Individual Psychology* 26, no. 3 (1990): 280–97.

33. See, for example, Meiselman, *Incest,* and McIntyre.

34. Aaron Hoorwitz, "Guidelines for Treating Father-Daughter Incest," *Social Casework* 64, no. 4 (1983): 515–24, esp. 515.

35. Karin Meiselman, *Incest,* 120.

36. Diane H. Browning and Bonny Boatman, "Incest: Children at Risk," *American Journal of Psychiatry* 134, no. 1 (1977): 69–72.

37. Judith Herman, *Father-Daughter Incest,* 79.

38. See the Ciba Foundation Report, *Child Sexual Abuse Within the Family* (New York: Tavistock, 1984).

39. Margaret Zuelzer and Richard Reposa, "Mothers in Incestuous Families," *International Journal of Family Therapy* 5 (1983): 99–108, esp. 104.

40. Grace Hubbard, "Mothers' Perceptions of Incest," 38.

41. Kathleen Coulborn Faller, "Why Sexual Abuse? An Exploration of the Intergenerational Hypothesis," *Child Abuse and Neglect* 13, no. 4 (1989): 543–48; Karin Meiselman, *Incest;* and Ronald L. Scott and David A. Stone, "MMPI Profile Constellations in Incest Families," *Journal of Consulting and Clinical Psychology* 54, no. 3 (1986): 364–68.

42. Judith Lewis Herman, *Trauma and Recovery: The Aftermath of Violence—From Domestic Abuse to Political Terror* (New York: Basic Books, 1992), 106.

3. Idealization of the Perpetrator

1. Juliet Mitchell, *Psychoanalysis and Feminism* (London: Allen Lane, 1974), 392.

2. Nancy Chodorow, *The Reproduction of Mothering: Psychoanalysis and the Sociology of Gender* (Berkeley: University of California Press, 1978); Susan Contratto, "Father Presence in Women's Psychological Development," in J. Rabow, ed., *Advances in Psychoanalytic Sociology: A Text and Reader* (Melbourne, FL.: Krieger, 1987), 139–55.

3. Robert Summit, "The Child Sexual Abuse Accommodation Syndrome," *Child Abuse and Neglect* 7 (1983): 177–93.

4. Jean Goodwin, "Post Traumatic Symptoms in Incest Victims," in Spencer Eth and Robert S. Pynoos, eds., *Post Traumatic Stress Disorder in Children* (Washington, D.C.: American Psychiatric Press, 1988): 157–68; Judith Lewis Herman, *Trauma and Recovery: The Aftermath of Violence—From Domestic Abuse to Political Terror* (New York: Basic Books, 1992).

5. For a discussion of repression, see Anna Freud, *The Ego and the Mechanism of Defense* (New York: International Universities Press, 1946).

6. Ibid.

7. Karin Meiselman, *Resolving the Trauma of Incest* (San Francisco: Jossey-Bass, 1990).

8. The demonization of the perpetrator, as it is discussed here, is distinguished from reports of ritual abuse and satanic cult practices. None of the respondents in this study reported having been ritually abused.

9. Written communication from Cordelia Candelaria, March 3, 1993.

10. Interview with Catherine Schieve, Denver, CO, February 19, 1993.

11. H.R. Trever Roper, *The European Witchcraze of the Sixteenth and Seventeenth Centuries and Other Essays* (New York: Harper and Row, 1967).

12. Judith Herman, *Trauma and Recovery*; and Jeffrey Moussaieff Masson, *The Assault on the Truth: Freud's Suppression of the Seduction Theory* (Farrar, Straus & Giroux, 1984).

13. Sigmund Freud, *The Origins of Psychoanalysis. Letters to Wilhelm Fliess, Drafts and Notes: 1887–1902*, ed. Marie Bonaparte, Anna Freud, and Ernst Kris, trans. Erans E. Mosbacher and James Strachey (New York: Basic Books, 1954), 187–88.

14. Judith Herman, *Trauma and Recovery*, 96.

15. Jeffrey Masson, *The Assault on Truth*.

16. Sigmund Freud, "A Seventeenth-Century Demonological Neurosis," *The Standard Edition of the Complete Psychological Works* Vol. 19 (London: The Hogarth Press, 1961), 86.

17. Judith Herman, *Trauma and Recovery*; Karin Meiselman, *Resolving the Trauma of Incest*.

18. Meiselman, Ibid.

19. Patricia Perri Rieker and Elaine Hilberman Carmen, "The Victim-To-Patient Process: The Disconfirmation and Transformation of Abuse," *American Journal of Orthopsychiatry* 56, no. 3 (1986): 360–64, esp. 362.

20. Judith Lewis Herman, *Father-Daughter Incest* (Cambridge, MA: Harvard University Press, 1981).

21. Christine A. Courtois, *Healing the Incest Wound: Adult Survivors in Therapy* (New York: W.W. Norton, 1988), 35.

22. Karen Marie Christa Minns, "Et Cuno Spiritu Tuo," in Toni A. H. McNaron and Yarrow Morgan, eds., *Voices in the Night: Women Speaking About Incest* (Pittsburgh, PA: Cleis Press, 1982): 23–29.

23. Gloria Anzaldua, "Entering Into the Serpent," in Judith Plaskow and Carol Christ, eds., *Weaving the Vision* (New York: Harper and Row, 1989), 77–86.

24. Ibid.

25. Cherrie Moraga, *Loving in the War Years* (Boston: South End, 1983), 118.

26. Patricia Hill Collins, *Black Feminist Thought* (Cambridge, MA: Unwin Hyman, 1990); and Angela Davis, "Rape, Racism and the Capitalist Setting," *Black Scholar* 9, no. 7 (1978): 24–30.

27. Patricia Hill Collins, *Black Feminist Thought*, 177.

28. Carolyn I. Thornton and James H. Carter, "Treatment Considerations with Black Incestuous Families," *Journal of the National Medical Association* 78, no. 1 (1986): 49–53, esp. 50.

29. Ibid.

30. Ibid., 49–50.

31. Louise Wisechild, *The Obsidian Mirror* (Seattle, WA: Seal Press, 1988), 83–85.

32. Annie Imbent and Ineke Jorker, *Christianity and Incest*, trans. Patricia McVay (Minneapolis, MN: Fortress Press, 1992): XIV.

33. Judith Herman, *Trauma and Recovery*, 105.

34. Angela Browne and David Finkelhor, "Impact of Child Sexual Abuse: A Review of the Research," *Psychological Bulletin* 99, no. 1 (1986): 66–77; J. James and J. Meyerding, "Early Sexual Experiences and Prostitution," *American Journal of Psychiatry* 134

(1977): 1381–85; Florence Rush, *The Best Kept Secret: Sexual Abuse of Children* (Englewood Cliffs, N.J.: Prentice-Hall, 1980).

35. Ellen Pillard, "Entering Prostitution: A Study Using the Narratives of Women," unpublished paper.

36. Judith Herman, *Trauma and Recovery*, 103.

4. Sexual Violence and the Empathic Female Self

1. See the collection of work from the Stone Center published in Judith V. Jordan, Alexandra G. Kaplan, Jean Baker Miller, Irene P. Stiver, and Janet L. Surrey, *Women's Growth in Connection: Writings from the Stone Center* (New York and London: The Guilford Press, 1991).

2. Carol Gilligan, *In A Different Voice* (Cambridge, MA: Harvard University Press, 1982); Evelyn Fox Keller, *Reflections on Gender and Science* (New Haven, CT: Yale University Press, 1985); Lillian Rubin, *Intimate Strangers* (New York: Harper and Row, 1983).

3. See, for example, Jean Baker Miller, "The Development of Women's Sense of Self," 11–26; and Judith V. Jordan, "Empathy and Self Boundaries," 67–80 in *Women's Growth in Connection* (note 1 above).

4. Judith V. Jordan, "Empathy and Self Boundaries," 69.

5. Janet L. Surrey, "The Self-in-Relation: A Theory of Women's Development," in *Women's Growth in Connection*, 56.

6. For a discussion of male entitlement and theories of female relationality, see Marcia Westkott, *The Feminist Legacy of Karen Horney* (New Haven and London: Yale University Press, 1986), 125–31.

7. Carol Tavris and Carole Offir, *The Longest War: Sex Differences in Perspective* (New York: Harcourt Brace Jovanovich, 1977).

8. Judith Jordan, "Empathy and Self Boundaries," 69.

9. Roy Schafer, *Aspects of Internalization* (New York: International Universities Press, 1968).

10. Jean Miller, "The Development of Women's Sense of Self," 13–14.

11. Nancy Chodorow, "Family Structure and Feminine Personality," in Michelle Rosaldo and Louise Lamphere, eds., *Woman, Culture and Society* (Palo Alto, CA: Stanford University Press, 1974), 43–66; Nancy Chodorow, *The Reproduction of Mothering: Psychoanalysis and the Sociology of Gender* (Berkeley: University of California Press, 1978); Dorothy Dinnerstein, *The Mermaid and the Minotaur* (New York: Harper and Row, 1976).

12. Janet Surrey, "The Self in Relation," 56.

13. Jessica Benjamin, *The Bonds of Love: Psychoanalysis, Feminism, and the Problem of Domination* (New York: Pantheon, 1988); Shulamith Firestone, *The Dialectic of Sex* (New York: Bantam, 1971).

14. Jessica Benjamin, *The Bonds of Love*.

15. Jeanne H. Block, "Another Look at Sex Differentiation in the Socialization Behaviors of Mothers and Fathers," in *The Psychology of Women: Future Directions of Research* (New York: Psychology Dimensions, 1978), 31–87; Miriam M. Johnson, "Fathers, Mothers, and Sex Typing," *Sociological Inquiry* 45, no. 1 (1975): 15–26.

16. Herbert Barry, Margaret Bacon, and Irvin Child, "A Cross Cultural Survey of Some Sex Differences in Socialization," *Journal of Abnormal Social Psychology* 55 (1957): 327–33.

17. Miriam Johnson, "Fathers, Mothers, and Sex Typing."

18. Michele Wallace, *Black Macho and the Myth of the Superwoman* (New York: Warner Books, 1978), 130–31.

19. Marcia Westkott, *The Feminist Legacy of Karen Horney*.

20. Ibid., 127.

21. Maya Angelou, *I Know Why the Caged Bird Sings* (New York: Bantam, 1970), 65.

22. R.C., "Remembering Dreams," in Ellen Bass and Louise Thornton, eds., *I Never Told Anyone: Writings by Women of Child Sexual Abuse* (New York: Harper and Row, 1983), 105–106.

23. Brendan MacCarthy, "Are Incest Victims Hated," *Psychoanalytic Psychotherapy* 3, no. 2 (1988): 115.

24. Jean Monroe, "From California Daughter," in Ellen Bass and Louise Thornton, eds., *I Never Told Anyone* (New York: Harper and Row, 1983), 93.

25. See Judith V. Jordan, "Empathy and Self Boundaries," for a discussion of empathic development in children and the impact of gender on empathy and personality formation.

26. Nancy Chodorow, "Family Structure and Feminine Personality," 59.

27. Judith Lewis Herman, *Father-Daughter Incest* (Cambridge, MA: Harvard University Press, 1981); and Marcia Westkott, *The Feminist Legacy of Karen Horney*.

28. Noel Lustig, John W. Dresser, Seth W. Spellman, and Thomas A. Murray, "Incest: A Family Group Survival Pattern," *Archives of General Psychiatry* 14 (1966): 31–40.

29. Judith Herman, *Father-Daughter Incest*, 83.

30. Alice Miller, *Thou Shalt Not Be Aware: Society's Betrayal of the Child* (New York: Farrar, Strauss & Giroux, 1984), 162.

31. Marcia Westkott, *The Feminist Legacy of Karen Horney*.

32. Judith Herman, *Father-Daughter Incest*.

33. Margaret L. Duncombe, "The Mother-Daughter Relationship in Father-Daughter Incest Families," paper presented at the National Women Studies Association Meetings, Towson State University, Townson, Maryland, June 1989.

34. Judith Herman, *Father-Daughter Incest*.

35. David Finkelhor, et al., *A Sourcebook on Childhood Sexual Abuse* (Beverly Hills, CA: Sage, 1986); Diana E.H. Russell, *The Secret Trauma: Incest in the Lives of Girls and Women* (New York: Basic Books, 1986); and Gail E. Wyatt and Gloria J. Powell,

Lasting Effects of Child Sexual Abuse (Beverly Hills, CA: Sage, 1988).

36. Judith Jordan, "Empathy and Self Boundaries."

37. Judith Lewis Herman, *Trauma and Recovery: The Aftermath of Violence—From Domestic Abuse to Political Terror* (New York: Basic Books, 1992).

38. Jean Baker Miller, "Connections, Disconnections and Violations," Work in Progress Collection (Wellesley, MA: Stone Center for Developmental Services and Studies, 1988), 10.

39. Ibid.

5. Identification with the Aggressor

1. Sandor Ferenczi, *Final Contributions to the Problems and Methods of Psycho-analysis* (London: The Hogarth Press, 1955), 156–67.

2. Ibid.

3. Ibid., 161.

4. Ibid., 162–63.

5. Nancy Chodorow, *The Reproduction of Mothering: Psychoanalysis and the Sociology of Gender* (Berkeley: University of California Press, 1978).

6. Jessica Benjamin, *The Bonds of Love: Psychoanalysis, Feminism, and the Problem of Domination* (New York: Pantheon, 1988), 100.

7. Ibid., 111.

8. Roy Schafer, *Aspects of Internalization* (New York: International Universities Press, 1968).

9. E. Sue Blume, *Secret Survivors: Uncovering Incest and Its Aftereffects in Women* (New York: Ballantine, 1990), 85.

10. Maxine Hong Kingston, *The Woman Warrior* (New York: Vintage, 1976), 23–4.

11. Ibid., 36.

12. Sigmund Freud, *New Introductory Lectures on Psychoanalysis,*

trans. James Strachey (New York: W.W. Norton, 1965).

13. Karen Horney, "On the Genesis of the Castration Complex in Women," in Harold Kelman, ed., *Feminine Psychology* (New York: W.W. Norton, 1967), 35–53; and "Der Mannlich Keitscomplex der Frau," ("The Masculinity Complex in Women") *Archive fur Fravenjunde* 13 (1927): 141–54.

14. Karen Horney, "The Masculinity Complex in Women," 148.

15. Ibid.

16. Karen Horney, "On the Genesis of the Castration Complex in Women," 50.

17. Nancy Chodorow, *The Reproduction of Mothering*.

18. Claire J. Aiosa-Karpas, Robert Karpas, David Pelcovitz, and Sandra Kaplan, "Gender Identification and Sex Role Attribution in Sexually Abused Adolescent Females," *Journal of the Academy of Child Adolescent Psychiatry* 30, no. 2 (1991): 266–71.

19. Roy Schafer, *Aspects of Internalization*.

20. Ellen Bass and Laura Davis, *The Courage to Heal* (New York: Harper and Row, 1988); Julien Bigras, "Father-Daughter Incest: 25 years of Experience of Psychoanalytic Psychotherapy with the Victims," *Canadian Journal of Psychiatry* 34, no. 8 (1989): 804–06; Margaret L. Duncombe, "Eating Disturbance and the Dependent Character Solution: Some Effects of Sexualizing and Devaluing Experience," unpublished paper; and J. Kinzl and W. Biebl, "Sexual Abuse of Girls: Aspects of the Genesis of Mental Disorders and Therapeutic Implications," *Acta Psychiatrica Scandinavica* 83 (1991): 427–31.

21. Ellen Bass and Laura Davis point out that bulimia (compulsive vomiting) in incest survivors may be a direct manifestation of the sexual assault, as vomiting is an unconscious attempt to expel the intrusive objects (fingers, penises, or other objects) from the body, especially if the abuse involved oral rape (see Bass and Davis, *The Courage to Heal*).

22. Jane M. Ussher, *The Psychology of the Female Body* (New York: Routledge, 1989), 38–39.

23. Karen Horney, "The Masculinity Complex in Women," 152.

24. Elaine H. Carmen, Patricia P. Rieker, and Trudy Mills, "Victims of Violence and Psychiatric Illness," *American Journal of Psychiatry* 141, no. 3 (1984): 378–83; and Christine A. Courtois, *Healing the Incest Wound: Adult Survivors in Therapy* (New York: W.W. Norton, 1988).

25. Christine Courtois, *Healing the Incest Wound*, 301–02.

26. Anna Freud, *The Ego and the Mechanism of Defense* (New York: International Universities Press, 1946), 121.

27. Leonard Shengold, *Soul Murder: The Effects of Childhood Abuse and Deprivation* (New York: Ballantine Books, 1989), 29.

28. Ibid., 30.

29. Mark Dadds, Michelle Smith, and Yvonne Webber, "An Exploration of Family and Individual Profiles Following Father-Daughter Incest," *Child Abuse and Neglect* 15 (1991), 584.

30. Julian Bigas, Pierre Leichner, Michel Perreault, and Richard Lavoie, "Severe Paternal Sexual Abuse in Early Childhood and Systematic Aggression Against the Family and the Institution," *Canadian Journal of Psychiatry* 36 (1991): 527–29; and Perihan Aral Rosenthal and Marvin B. Doherty, "Psychodynamics of Delinquent Girls' Rage and Violence Directed Toward Mother," *Adolescent Psychiatry* 12 (1985): 281–89.

31. Susan Forward and Craig Buck, *Betrayal of Innocence* (New York: Penguin Books, 1979); Judith Lewis Herman, *Trauma and Recovery: The Aftermath of Violence—from Domestic Abuse to Political Terror* (New York: Basic Books, 1992); and Karin Meiselman, *Resolving the Trauma of Incest* (San Francisco: Jossey-Bass, 1990).

32. Susan Forward and Craig Buck, *Betrayal of Innocence*, 108.

33. Similar findings have been found cross-culturally. See, for example, Caroline Gluckman's work with a young Asian incest victim in London, England, reported in *Journal of Child Psychotherapy* 13, no. 1 (1987): 109–23.

6. Revictimization and the Divided Consciousness of Aggression and Abuse

1. E. Sue Blume, *Secret Survivors: Uncovering Incest and Its Aftereffects In Women* (New York: Ballantine, 1989); M.G. Runtz, "The Sexual Victimization of Women: The Link Between Child Abuse and Revictimization," paper presented at the annual meeting of the Canadian Psychological Association, Vancouver, B.C., 1987, cited in Christine A. Courtois, *Healing the Incest Wound: Adult Survivors in Therapy* (New York: W.W. Norton, 1988); Diana E.H. Russell, *The Secret Trauma: Incest in the Lives of Girls and Women* (New York: Basic Books, 1986); and Lenore E. Walker, *The Battered Woman Syndrome* (New York: Springer, 1984).

2. Diana Russell, *The Secret Trauma*.

3. M.G. Runtz, "The Sexual Victimization of Women."

4. Alvin A. Rosenfeld, "Endogamic Incest and the Victim-Perpetrator Model," *American Journal of Diseases of Children* 133 (1979): 406–10.

5. Lenore Walker, *The Battered Woman Syndrome*.

6. Christine Courtois, *Healing the Incest Wound*, 78.

7. Bessel A. van der Kolk, "The Compulsion to Repeat the Trauma: Re-enactment, Revictimization, and Masochism," *Psychiatric Clinics of North America* 12, no. 2 (1989): 389–411, esp. 396.

8. Ibid.

9. For a discussion of repetition compulsion in the therapeutic setting, see Julien Bigras, "Father-Daughter Incest: 25 Years of Experience of Psychoanalytic Psychotherapy with the Victims," *Canadian Journal of Psychiatry* 34, no. 8 (1989): 804–06.

10. Paula J. Caplan, *The Myth of Women's Masochism* (New York: E.P. Dutton, 1985).

11. Ibid., 35–36.

12. Linda Phelps, "Female Sexual Alienation," in Jo Freeman, ed., *Women: A Feminist Perspective* (Palo Alto, CA: Mayfield, 1979): 18–26, esp. 22.

13. Martin S. Weinberg, Colin J. Williams, and Charles C. Moser, "The Social Constituents of Sadomasochism," *Social Problems* 31, no. 4 (1984): 379–89.

14. Jessica Benjamin, *The Bonds of Love: Psychoanalysis, Feminism, and the Problem of Domination* (New York: Pantheon, 1988), 69.

7. The Body as Self

1. Jessica Benjamin, *The Bonds of Love: Psychoanalysis, Feminism, and the Problem of Domination* (New York: Pantheon, 1988); and Jane M. Ussher, *The Psychology of the Female Body* (New York: Routledge, 1989).

2. Angela Browne and David Finkelhor, "Impact of Child Sexual Abuse: A Review of the Research," *Psychological Bulletin* 99, no. 1 (1986): 66–77; and Alvin A. Rosenfeld, "Endogamic Incest and the Victim-Perpetrator Model," *American Journal of Diseases of Children* 133 (1979): 406–10.

3. Judith Lewis Herman, *Father-Daughter Incest* (Cambridge, MA: Harvard University Press, 1981), 98.

4. E. Sue Blume, *Secret Survivors: Uncovering Incest and Its Aftereffects in Women* (New York: Ballantine, 1990), 122.

5. Sandor Ferenczi, *Final Contributions to the Problems and Methods of Psychoanalysis* (London: The Hogarth Press, 1955), 162.

6. Alice Miller, *Thou Shalt Not Be Aware: Society's Betrayal of the Child* trans. Hildegarde Hannum and Hunter Hannum (New York: Farrar, Straus & Giroux, 1984), 42.

7. Ibid.

8. Darlene Bregman Ehrenberg, "Abuse and Desire: A Case of Father-Daughter Incest," *Contemporary Psychoanalysis* 23, no. 4 (1987), 595.

9. Jessica Benjamin, *Bonds of Love*, 131–32.

10. E. Sue Blume, *Secret Survivors*.

11. Christine A. Courtois, *Healing the Incest Wound: Adult Surivors in Therapy* (New York: W.W. Norton, 1988), 153–55.

12. Wendy Maltz and Beverly Holman, *Incest and Sexuality: A Guide to Understanding and Healing* (Lexington, MA: D.C. Heath, 1987), 34.

13. Christine Courtois, *Healing the Incest Wound*, 155.

14. For a discussion of diverse types of dissociative disorders, see Christine Courtois, *Healing the Incest Wound*, 154–59.

15. Leonard Shengold, *Soul Murder: The Effects of Childhood Abuse and Deprivation* (New York: Ballantine, 1989), 142.

16. Ellen Bass and Laura Davis, *The Courage to Heal: A Guide for Women Survivors of Child Sexual Abuse* (New York: Harper and Row, 1988), 76.

17. Wendy Maltz and Beverly Holman, *Incest and Sexuality*, esp. chapter 8.

8. Change and Transformation: Reconstructing the Female Self

1. Ellen Bass and Laura Davis, *The Courage to Heal: A Guide For Women Survivors of Child Sexual Abuse* (New York: Harper and Row, 1988).

2. Christine Dinsmore, *From Surviving to Thriving: Incest, Feminism and Recovery* (Albany, NY: State University of New York Press, 1991).

3. Judith Lewis Herman, *Trauma and Recovery: The Aftermath of Violence—From Domestic Abuse to Political Terror* (New York: Basic Books, 1992); and Leonard Shengold, *Soul Murder: The Effects of Childhood Abuse and Deprivation* (New York: Ballantine, 1989).

4. Caroline Gluckman, "Incest in Psychic Reality," *Journal of Child Psychotherapy* 13, no. 1 (1987): 109–23.

5. William Butler Yeats, *The Poems of W. B. Yeats*, Richard J. Finneran, ed. (New York: Macmillan, 1956), 214–15.

6. Leonard Shengold, *Soul Murder*.

7. Judith Herman, *Trauma and Recovery*, 206.

8. Ellen Bass and Laura Davis, *The Courage to Heal*, 264.

9. Judith Herman points out that in therapy the identification with the aggressor often becomes apparent in traumatic transference, whereby the perpetrator's aggression, as manifested in the personality of the survivor, "intrudes repeatedly into the relationship between therapist and patient." See Judith Herman, *Trauma and Recovery*, 136.

10. Judith Herman, *Trauma and Recovery*.

11. For a discussion of feminism and spirituality, see Judith Plaskow and Carol Christ, eds., *Weaving the Vision* (New York: Harper & Row, 1989).

12. Francis Wesley, "Ritual as Psychic Bridge Building," *Journal of Psychoanalytic Anthropology* 6 (1983): 179–200.

13. Kathie Carlson, *In Her Image: The Unhealed Daughter's Search for Her Mother* (Boston: Shambala, 1989), 98.

14. Janet L. Jacobs, "The Effects of Ritual Healing on Female Victims of Abuse: A Study of Empowerment and Transformation," *Sociological Analysis* 50, no. 3 (1989), 274.

15. Ibid.

16. Alice Miller, *Thou Shalt Not Be Aware: Society's Betrayal of the Child* trans. Hildegarde Hannum and Hunter Hannum (New York: Farrar, Straus & Giroux, 1984).

17. Louise DeSalvo, *Virginia Woolf: The Impact of Childhood Sexual Abuse on Her Life and Work* (Boston: Beacon, 1989); and Diane Wood Middlebrook, *Anne Sexton: A Biography* (Boston: Houghton Mifflin, 1991).

18. *Selected Poems of Anne Sexton*, ed. Diane Wood Middlebrook and Diane Humes (Boston: Houghton Mifflin, 1988), 173.

19. Ellen Bass and Louise Thornton, eds., *I Never Told Anyone: Writings by Women of Child Sexual Abuse* (New York: Harper and Row, 1983); Toni A.H. NcNaron and Yarrow Morgan, eds.,

Voices in the Night: Women Speaking About Incest (Pittsburgh, PA: Cleis, 1982).

20. Susan Chute, "Black Girl Learn the Holiness of Motherhood," *Voices in the Night,* 60.

21. *Voices in the Night,* 17–18.

Bibliography

Adams, Paul L. "Replacing and Renewing Family Subsystems When the Incestuous Father Departs." *The American Journal of Social Psychiatry* 7, no. 1 (1987): 13–18.

Aiosa-Karpas, Claire J., Robert Karpas, David Pelcovitz, and Sandra Kaplan. "Gender Identification and Sex Role Attribution in Sexually Abused Adolescent Females." *Journal of the Academy of Child Adolescent Psychiatry* 30, no. 2 (1991): 266–71.

Alexander, Pamela C., and Shirley Lupfer, "Family Characteristics and Long-Term Consequences Associated With Sexual Abuse." *Archives of Sexual Behavior* 16, no. 3 (1987): 235–45.

Angelou, Maya. *I Know Why the Caged Bird Sings* (New York: Bantam, 1970).

Arcana, Judith. *Our Mother's Daughters* (Berkeley: Shameless Hussy Press, 1979).

Arens, W. *The Original Sin: Incest and Its Meaning* (New York: Oxford University Press, 1986).

Biale, Rachel. *Women and the Jewish Law: An Exploration of Women's Issues in Halakhic Sources* (New York: Schocken Books, 1984).

Balint, Michael. *Primary Love and Psycho-Analytic Technique* (London: Tavistock, 1965).

Barry, Herbert, Margaret Bacon, and Irvin Child. "A Cross Cultural

Survey of Some Sex Differences in Socialization." *Journal of Abnormal Social Psychology* 55 (1957): 327–33.

Bass, Ellen, and Laura Davis. *The Courage to Heal: A Guide for Women Survivors of Child Sexual Abuse* (New York: Harper and Row, 1988).

Benjamin, Jessica. *The Bonds of Love: Psychoanalysis, Feminism, and the Problem of Domination* (New York: Pantheon, 1988).

Bigras, Julien. "Father-Daughter Incest: 25 years of Experience of Psychoanalytic Psychotherapy with the Victims." *Canadian Journal of Psychiatry* 34, no. 8 (1989): 804–06.

Bigras, Julien, Pierre Leichner, Michel Perreault, and Richard Lavoie. "Severe Paternal Sexual Abuse in Early Childhood and Systematic Aggression Against the Family and the Institution." *Canadian Journal of Psychiatry* 36 (1991): 527–29.

Block, Jeanne H. "Another Look at Sex Differentiation in the Socialization Behaviors of Mothers and Fathers." In *The Psychology of Women: Future Directions of Research* (New York: Psychology Dimensions, 1978), 31–87.

Blume, E. Sue. *Secret Survivors: Uncovering Incest and Its Aftereffects in Women* (New York: Ballantine Books, 1990).

Brooks, Barbara. "Familial Influences in Father-Daughter Incest." *Journal of Psychiatric Treatment and Evaluation* 4, no. 2 (1982): 117–124.

Browne, Angela, and David Finkelhor. "Impact of Child Sexual Abuse: A Review of the Research." *Psychological Bulletin* 99, no. 1 (1986): 66–77.

Browning, Diane H., and Bonny Boatman. "Incest: Children at Risk." *American Journal of Psychiatry* 134, no. 1 (1977): 69–72.

Brunngraber, Lee Stroessner. "Father Daughter Incest: Immediate and Long Term Effects of Sexual Abuse." *Advance in Nursing Science* 8, no. 4 (1986): 15–35.

Candelaria, Cordelia, "Malinche, Feminist Prototype." *Frontiers: A Journal of Women Studies* 5, no. 2 (1980): 1–6.

Caplan, Paula J. *The Myth of Women's Masochism* (New York: E.P. Dutton, 1985).

———. *Don't Blame Mother: Mending the Mother-Daughter Relationship* (New York: Harper and Row, 1989).

Carlson, Kathie. *In Her Image: The Unhealed Daughter's Search for Her Mother* (Boston: Shambala, 1989).

Carmen, Elaine H., Patricia P. Rieker, and Trudy Mills. "Victims of Violence and Psychiatric Illness." *American Journal of Psychiatry* 141, no.3 (1984): 378–83.

Chodorow, Nancy. *The Reproduction of Mothering: Psychoanalysis and the Sociology of Gender* (Berkeley: University of California Press, 1978).

———. "Family Structure and Feminine Personality." In *Woman, Culture and Society*, edited by Michelle Rosaldo and Louise Lamphere (Palo Alto, CA.: Stanford University Press, 1974), 43–66.

Chodorow, Nancy, and Susan Contratto. "The Fantasy of the Perfect Mother." In *Rethinking the Family: Some Feminist Questions*, edited by Barrie Thorne with Marilyn Yalom (New York: Longman, 1980), 54–75.

Ciba Foundation Report, *Child Sexual Abuse Within the Family* (New York: Tavistock, 1984).

Collins, Patricia Hill. *Black Feminist Thought* (Cambridge, MA: Unwin Hyman, 1990).

Collings, Steven J., and Payne F. Merrilee, "Attribution of Causal and Moral Responsibility to Victims of Father-Daughter Incest: An Exploratory Examination of Five Factors." *Child Abuse and Neglect* 15, no. 4 (1991): 513–521.

Contratto, Susan. "Father Presence in Women's Psychological Development." In *Advances in Psychoanalytic Sociology: A Text and Reader*, edited by J. Rabow (Melbourne, FL: Krieger, 1987), 139–55.

Courtois, Christine A. *Healing the Incest Wound: Adult Survivors in Therapy* (New York: W.W. Norton, 1988).

Dadds, Mark, Michelle Smith, and Yvonne Webber. "An Exploration of Family and Individual Profiles Following Father-Daughter Incest." *Child Abuse and Neglect* 15, no. 4 (1991), 584.

Davis, Angela. "Rape, Racism and the Capitalist Setting." *Black Scholar* 9, no. 7 (1978): 24–30.

deChesnay, Mary, Elaine Marshall, and Carol Clements, "Family Structure, Marital Power, Maternal Distance, and Paternal Alcohol Consumption in Father-Daughter Incest." *Family Systems Medicine* 6, No. 4 (1988): 453–62.

DeSalvo, Louise. *Virginia Woolf: The Impact of Childhood Sexual Abuse on Her Life and Work* (Boston: Beacon, 1989).

Dinnerstein, Dorothy. *The Mermaid and the Minotaur* (New York: Harper and Row, 1976).

Dinsmore, Christine. *From Surviving to Thriving: Incest, Feminism and Recovery* (Albany, NY.: State Univerity of New York Press, 1991).

Dominelli, Lena. "Father-Daughter Incest: Patriarchy's Shameful Secret." *Critical Social Policy* 6, no. 16 (1986): 8–22.

Emily Driver and Audrey Droisen, eds. *Child Sexual Abuse: Feminist Perspectives* (London: MacMillan Education LTD, 1989).

Duncombe, Margaret L. "Eating Disturbance and the Dependent Character Solution: Some Effects of Sexualizing and Devaluing Experience." Unpublished paper.

———. "The Mother-Daughter Relationship in Father-Daughter Incest Families." Paper presented at the National Women's Studies Association Meetings, Townsend, Maryland, June 1989.

Ehrenberg, Darlene Bregman. "Abuse and Desire: A Case of Father-Daughter Incest." *Contemporary Psychoanalysis* 23, no. 4 (1987), 595.

Ehrensaft, Diane. "When Women and Men Mother." In *Mothering: Essays in Feminist Theory*, edited by Joyce Treblicot (Totowa, NJ: Rowman and Allenheld, 1984), 41–61.

Everson, Mark D., Wanda M. Hunter, Desmond K. Runyon, Gail A. Edelsohn, and Martha L. Coulter. "Maternal Support Following Disclosure of Incest." *American Journal of Orthopsychiatry* 59 (1989), 197–207.

Engel, Beverly. *The Right to Innocence: Healing the Trauma of Sexual Abuse* (Los Angeles: Jeremy P. Tarcher, 1982).

Fairbairn, Ronald. *An Object Relations Theory of the Personality* (New York: Basic Books, 1952).

Faller, Kathleen Coulborn. "Why Sexual Abuse? An Exploration of the Intergenerational Hypothesis." *Child Abuse and Neglect* 13, no. 4 (1989): 543–48.

Farrell, Lynda T. "Factors That Affect a Victim's Self Disclosure in Father-Daughter Incest." *Child Welfare* 67, No. 5 (1988): 462–69.

Ferenczi, Sandor. *Final Contributions to the Problems and Methods of Psycho-analysis* (London: The Hogarth Press, 1955).

Feldstein, Richard, and Judith Roof, eds. *Feminism and Psychoanalysis* (Ithaca, NY: Cornell University Press, 1989).

Ferguson, Ann. "On Conceiving Motherhood and Sexuality: A Feminist Materialist Approach." In *Mothering: Essays in Feminist Theory* edited by Joyce Treblicot (Totowa, NJ: Rowman and Allenheld, 1984), 153–67.

Finkelhor, David. *Sexually Victimized Children* (New York: The Free Press, 1979).

Finkelhor, David, et al. *A Sourcebook on Childhood Sexual Abuse* (Beverly Hills, CA: Sage, 1986).

Firestone, Shulamith. *The Dialectic of Sex* (New York: Bantam, 1971).

Flax, Jane. *Thinking Fragments: Psychoanalysis, Feminism, and Postmodernism in the Contemporary West* (Berkeley: University of California Press, 1990).

Forward, Susan, and Craig Buck. *Betrayal of Innocence* (New York: Penguin Books, 1979).

Freud, Anna. *The Ego and the Mechanism of Defense* (New York: International Universities Press, 1946).

Freud, Sigmund. *Collected Papers, Vol. I*, trans. Joan Riviere (London: The Hogarth Press, 1945).

———. *The Origins of Psychoanalysis: Letters to Wilhelm Fliess*, eds. Marie Bonaparte, Anna Freud, and Ernst Kris, trans. Eric Mosbacher and James Strachey (New York: Basic Books, 1954).

————. *The Standard Edition of the Complete Psychological Works*, Vol. 14, trans. James Strachey (London: The Hogarth Press, 1958).

————. *The Standard Edition of the Complete Psychological Works*, Vol. 19, trans. James Strachey (London: The Hogarth Press, 1961).

————. *New Introductory Lectures on Psychoanalysis*, trans., James Strachey (New York: W.W. Norton, 1965).

Friday, Nancy. *My Mother My Self* (New York: Delacorte, 1977).

Frude, Neil, "The Sexual Nature of Sexual Abuse: A Review of the Literature." *Child Abuse and Neglect* 6, no. 4 (1982): 211–223.

Gardner, Shirley Nelson, Claire Kahane, and Madelon Sprengnether, eds. *The (M)other Tongue: Essays in Feminist Psychoanalytic Interpretation* (Ithaca and London: Cornell University Press, 1985).

Gil, Vincent E. "In Thy Father's House: Self Report Findings of Sexually Abused Daughters from Conservative Christian Homes." *Journal of Psychology and Theology* 16, No. 2 (1988): 144–152.

Gilligan, Carol. *In a Different Voice* (Cambridge, MA: Harvard University Press, 1982).

Gluckman, Caroline. "Incest in Psychic Reality." *Journal of Child Psychotherapy* 13, no. 1 (1987): 109–23.

Goodwin, Jean. "Post Traumatic Symptoms in Incest Victims." In *Post Traumatic Stress Disorder in Children*, edited by Spencer Eth and Robert S. Pynoos (Washington, D.C.: American Psychiatric Press, 1985): 157–68.

Gordon, Linda. *Heroes of Their Own Lives: The Politics and History of Family Violence* (New York: Viking, 1988).

Gordon, Linda, and Paul O'Keefe. "Incest as a Form of Family Violence: Evidence from Historical Case Records." *Journal of Marriage and Family* 46, no. 1 (1984): 27–34.

Herman, Judith Lewis. *Father-Daughter Incest* (Cambridge, MA: Harvard University Press, 1981).

————. *Trauma and Recovery: The Aftermath of Violence—From Domestic Abuse to Political Terror* (New York: Basic Books, 1992).

Herman, Judith Lewis, and Lisa Hirshman. "Father-Daughter Incest."

In *Signs Reader*, edited by Elizabeth Abel and Emily F. Abel (Chicago: University of Chicago Press, 1983): 257–58.

Hirschhorn, Norbert. "A Bandaged Secret: Emily Dickinson and Incest." *The Journal of Psychohistory* 8, no. 3 (1991): 251–81.

Hoorwitz, Aaron. "Guidelines for Treating Father-Daughter Incest." *Social Casework* 64, no. 4 (1983): 515–24.

Horney, Karen. "Der Mannlich Keitscomplex der Frau" ("The Masculinity Complex in Women.") *Archive fur Fravenjunde* 13 (1927): 141–54.

———. *Feminine Psychology*, edited by Harold Kelman (New York: W.W. Norton, 1967).

Hubbard, Grace B. "Mothers' Perceptions of Incest: Sustained Disruption and Turmoil." *Archives of Psychiatric Nursing* 3, no. 1 (1989): 34–40.

Hyde, Naida D. "Covert Incest in Women's Lives: Dynamics and Directions for Healing." *Canadian Journal for Community Mental Health* 5, no. 2 (1986): 73–83.

Imbent, Annie, and Ineke Jorker. *Christianity and Incest*, trans. Patricia McVay (Minneapolis, MN: Fortress, 1992).

Jacobs, Janet L. "The Effects of Ritual Healing on Female Victims of Abuse: A Study of Empowerment and Transformation." *Sociological Analysis* 50, no. 3 (1989): 265–79.

James, J., and J. Meyerding, "Early Sexual Experiences and Prostitution." *American Journal of Psychiatry* 134 (1977): 1381–385.

James, Kerri, and Lauri Mackinnon, "The 'Incestuous Family' Revisited: A Critical Analysis of Family Therapy Myths." *Journal of Marital and Family Therapy* 16, no. 1 (1990): 71–88.

Johnson, Miriam M. "Fathers, Mothers, and Sex Typing." *Sociological Inquiry* 45, no. 1 (1975): 15–26.

———. "Heterosexuality, Male Dominance, and the Father Image." *Sociological Inquiry* 51, no. 2 (1981): 129–39.

Jordan, Judith V., Alexandra G. Kaplan, Jean Baker Miller, Irene P. Stiver, and Janet L. Surrey, *Women's Growth in Connection: Writings from the Stone Center* (New York and London: The Guilford Press, 1991).

Keller, Evelyn Fox. *Reflections on Gender and Science* (New Haven, CT: Yale University Press, 1985).

Kempe, Ruth, and C. Henry Kempe, *The Common Secret: Sexual Abuse of Children and Adolescents* (New York: W.H. Freeman, 1984).

Kingston, Maxine Hong. *The Woman Warrior* (New York: Vintage, 1976).

Kinzl, J., and W. Biebl. "Sexual Abuse of Girls: Aspects of the Genesis of Mental Disorders and Therapeutic Implications." *Acta Psychiatrica Scandinavica* 83 (1991): 427–31.

Kirkland, Karen D., and Chris Bauer, "MMPI Traits of Incestuous Fathers." *Journal of Clinical Psychology* 38, no. 3 (1982): 645–49.

Koch, Kathleen, and Carolyn Jarvis, "Symbiotic Mother-Daughter Relationships in Incest Families." *Social Casework: The Journal of Contemporary Social Work* (February 1987): 94–101.

van der Kolk, Bessel A. "The Compulsion to Repeat the Trauma: Re-enactment, Revictimization, and Masochism." *Psychiatric Clinics of North America* 12, no. 2 (1989): 384–411.

LaBarbera, Joseph D. "Seductive Father-Daughter Relationships and Sex Roles in Women." *Sex Roles* 11, no. 9/10 (1984): 941–51.

Leonard, Marjorie. "Fathers and Daughters: The Significance of 'Fathering' in the Psychosexual Development of the Girl." *International Journal of Psychoanalysis* 47 (1966): 325–34.

Lindholm, Kathryn J., and Richard Wiley, "Ethnic Differences in Child and Sexual Abuse." *Hispanic Journal of Behavioral Sciences* 8, no. 2 (1986): 111–25.

Lorde, Audre. *Sister Outsider* (New York: The Crossing Press, 1984).

Lustig, Noel, John W. Dresser, Seth W. Spellman, and Thomas A. Murray. "Incest: A Family Group Survival Pattern." *Archives of General Psychiatry* 14 (1966): 31–40.

MacCarthy, Brendan. "Are Incest Victims Hated." *Psychoanalytic Psychotherapy* 3, no. 2 (1988): 115.

McCleer, Susan V., Esther Deblinger, Marc S. Atkins, Edna B. Foa, and Diana L. Ralphe, "Post Traumatic Stress Disorder in Sexually Abused Children." *Journal of the American Academy of Child and Adolescent Psychiatry* 27, no. 5 (1988): 650–54.

MacFarlane, Kee, and Jill Waterman, *The Sexual Abuse of Young Children* (New York: The Guilford Press, 1986).

McIntosh, Mary. "Introduction to an Issue: Family Secret as Public Drama." *Feminist Review* 28 (1988): 6–15.

McIntyre, Kevin. "Role of Mothers in Father-Daughter Incest: A Feminist Analysis." *Social Work* 26 (1981): 462–66.

MacLeod, Mary, and Esther Saraga. "Challenging the Orthodoxy: Towards a Feminist Theory and Practice," *Feminist Review* 28 (1988): 16–55.

McNaron, Toni A.H., and Yarrow Morgan, eds. *Voices in the Night: Women Speaking About Incest* (Pittsburgh, PA: Cleis, 1982).

Maltz, Wendy, and Beverly Holman. *Incest and Sexuality: A Guide to Understanding and Healing* (Lexington, MA: D.C. Heath, 1987).

Marquez, Stephanie Amedeo, "The Hidden Victim's Cry of Fury: The Imagery of Incest and Sylvia Plath's 'Daddy.'" Paper presented at the Western Social Science Association Meeting, April 1992, Denver, Colorado.

Masson, Jeffrey Moussaieff. *The Assault on Truth: Freud's Suppression of the Seduction Theory* (New York: Farrar, Straus & Giroux, 1984).

Meiselman, Karin. *Incest: A Psychological Study of Causes and Effects with Treatment Recommendations* (San Francisco: Jossey-Bass, 1978).

———. *Resolving the Trauma of Incest* (San Francisco: Jossey-Bass, 1990).

Middlebrook, Diane Wood. *Anne Sexton: A Biography* (Boston: Houghton Mifflin, 1991).

Miller, Alice. *Thou Shalt Not Be Aware: Society's Betrayal of the Child*, trans. Hildegarde Hannum and Hunter Hannum (New York: Farrar, Straus & Giroux, 1984).

Miller, Jean Baker. *Toward a New Psychology of Women* (Boston: Beacon Press, 1986).

————. "Connections, Disconnections and Violations." Work in Progress Collection (Wellesley, MA: Stone Center for Developmental Services and Studies, 1988).

Mitchell, Juliet. *Women's Estate* (New York: Pantheon, 1971).

————. *Psychoanalysis and Feminism* (London: Allen Lane, 1974).

Moraga, Cherrie. *Loving in the War Years* (Boston: South End, 1983).

Myer, Margaret H. "A New Look at Mothers of Incest Victims." *Journal of Social Work and Human Sexuality* 3, nos. 2–3 (1984–5): 47–58.

Passey, Linda S. "Behavior Leading to Father-Daughter Incest: A Further Test of the Warner-Kearney Hypothesis." Paper presented at the Western Social Science Association Meeting, April 1987, Albuquerque, New Mexico.

Phelps, Linda. "Female Sexual Alienation." In *Women: A Feminist Perspective*, edited by Jo Freeman (Palo Alto, CA: Mayfield, 1979): 18–26.

Pierce, Robert, and Lois Pierce. "Child Sexual Abuse: A Black Perspective." In *Violence in the Black Family*, edited by Robert L. Hampton (Lexington, MA: Lexington, 1987), 67–85.

Pillard, Ellen. "Entering Prostitution: A Study Using the Narratives of Women." Unpublished paper.

Plaskow, Judith, and Carol Christ, eds. *Weaving the Vision* (New York: Harper and Row, 1989).

Renvoize, Jean. *Incest: A Family Pattern* (New York and London: Routledge, 1982).

Rich, Adrienne. *Of Woman Born* (New York: W.W. Norton, 1976).

Rieker, Patricia Perri, and Elaine Hilberman Carmen. "The Victim-To-Patient Process: The Disconfirmation and Transformation of Abuse." *American Journal of Orthopsychiatry* 56, no. 3 (1986): 360–64.

Roland, Billy, Paul Zelhart, and Richard Dubes. "MMPI Correlates of College Women Who Reported Experiencing Child/Adult Sexual Contact With Father, Stepfather, or With Other Persons." *Psychological Reports* 64 (1989): 1159–1162.

Roper, H.R. Trever. *The European Witchcraze of the Sixteenth and Seventeenth Centuries and Other Essays* (New York: Harper and Row, 1967).

Rosenfeld, Alvin A. "Endogamic Incest and the Victim-Perpetrator Model." *American Journal of Diseases of Children* 133 (1979): 406–10.

Rosenthal, Perihan Aral, and Marvin B. Doherty. "Psychodynamics of Delinquent Girls' Rage and Violence Directed Toward Mother." *Adolescent Psychiatry* 12 (1985): 281–89.

Rubin, Gayle. "The Traffic in Women." In *Toward an Anthropology of Women*, edited by Rayna R. Reiter (New York: Monthly Press, 1975), 157–210.

Rubin, Lillian. *Intimate Strangers* (New York: Harper and Row, 1983).

Rucker, Naomi G., and Karen L. Lombardi. "The Familial Menage-a-Trois: Mother-Daughter Sexuality and Father-Daughter Incest." *Journal of Contemporary Psychotherapy* 20, no.2 (1990): 99–107.

Ruether, Rosemary Radford. *Womanguides: Readings Toward A Feminist Theology* (Boston: Beacon, 1985).

Rush, Florence. *The Best Kept Secret: Sexual Abuse of Children* (Englewood Cliffs, NJ: Prentice-Hall, 1980).

Russell, Diana E.H. "The Incidence and Prevalence of Intrafamilial and Extrafamilial Sexual Abuse of Female Children." *Child Abuse and Neglect* 7, no. 2 (1983): 133–46.

———. *The Secret Trauma: Incest in the Lives of Girls and Women* (New York: Basic Books, 1986).

Sayers, Janet. *Sexual Contradictions: Psychology, Psychoanalysis, and Feminism* (London: Tavistock, 1986).

Schafer, Roy. *Aspects of Internalization* (New York: International Universities Press, 1968).

Scott, Ronald L., and David A. Stone. "MMPI Profile Constellations in Incest Families." *Journal of Consulting and Clinical Psychology* 54, no. 3 (1986): 364–68.

Selby, James W., Lawrence G. Calhoun, Joanne M. Jones, and Lisolette Matthews, "Families of Incest: A Collation of Clinical Impressions."

International Journal of Social Psychiatry 26, no. 1 (1980): 7–16.

Sexton, Anne. *Selected Poems of Anne Sexton* edited by Diane Wood Middlebrook and Diane Humes (Boston: Houghton Mifflin, 1988).

Shapiro, Shanti. "Self Mutilation and Self Blame in Incest Victims." *American Journal of Psychotherapy* 41, no. 1 (1987): 46–54.

Shengold, Leonard. *Soul Murder: The Effects of Childhood Abuse and Deprivation* (New York: Ballantine, 1989).

Sleeth, Pamela, and Jan Barnsley. *Recollecting Our Lives* (Vancouver: Press Gang, 1989).

Strand, Virginia. "Treatment of the Mother in the Incest Family: The Beginning Phase." *Clinical Social Work Journal* 18, no. 4 (1990): 353–65.

Summit, Robert. "The Child Sexual Abuse Accommodation Syndrome." *Child Abuse and Neglect* 7 (1983): 177–93.

Tavris, Carol, and Carole Offir. *The Longest War: Sex Differences in Perspective* (New York: Harcourt Brace Jovanovich, 1977).

Thornton, Carolyn I., and James H. Carter. "Treatment Considerations With Black Incestuous Families." *Journal of the National Medical Association* 78, no. 1 (1986): 49–53.

Tinling, Lydia. "Perpetuation of Incest by Significant Others: Mothers Who Do Not Want to See." *Individual Psychology* 26, no. 3 (1990): 280–97.

Truesdall, Donna L., John S. McNeil, and Jeanne P. Deschner, "Incidence of Wife Abuse in Incestuous Families." *Social Work* 31, no. 21 (1986): 138–40.

Ussher, Jane M. *The Psychology of the Female Body* (New York: Routledge, 1989).

Walker, Alice. *In Search of Our Mothers' Gardens* (New York: Harcourt, Brace, Jovanovich, 1983).

Walker, Lenore E. *The Battered Woman Syndrome* (New York: Springer, 1984).

Wallace, Michele. *Black Macho and the Myth of the Superwoman* (New York: Warner, 1978).

Wattenberg, Esther. "In a Different Light: A Feminist Perspective on the Role of Mothers in Father-Daughter Incest." *Child Welfare* 64, no. 3 (1985): 203–11.

Weinberg, Martin S., Colin J. Williams, and Charles C. Moser. "The Social Constituents of Sadomasochism." *Social Problems* 31, no. 4 (1984): 379–89.

Wesley, Francis. "Ritual as Psychic Bridge Building." *Journal of Psychoanalytic Anthropology* 6 (1983): 179–200.

Westkott, Marcia. *The Feminist Legacy of Karen Horney* (New Haven and London: Yale University Press, 1986).

Winnicott, Donald. *Collected Papers* (London: Tavistock, 1958).

Wisechild, Louise. *The Obsidian Mirror* (Seattle, WA: Seal Press, 1988).

Wolfe, David A., and Peter Jaffe, "Child Abuse and Family Violence as Determinants of Child Psychopathology." *Canadian Journal of Behavioral Science* 23, no. 3 (1991): 282–99.

Wolfe, Vicky V., Carole Gentell, and David A. Wolfe. "The Impact of Sexual Abuse on Children: A PTSD Formulation." *Behavior Therapy* 20, no. 2 (1989): 215–28.

Wolff, Larry. *Postcards from the End of the World: Child Abuse in Freud's Vienna* (New York: Atheneum, 1988).

Wyatt, Gail E., and Gloria J. Powell. *Lasting Effects of Child Sexual Abuse* (Beverly Hills, CA: Sage, 1988).

Yeats, William Butler. *The Poems of W. B. Yeats*, Richard J. Finneran, ed. (New York: Macmillan, 1956).

Zuelzer, Margaret, and Richard Reposa. "Mothers in Incestuous Families." *International Journal of Family Therapy* 5 (1983): 99–108.

Index